Bloom!

Bloom!

SERVING GOD
WHERE HE HAS PLANTED YOU

Elaine Hersman

REDEMPTION
PRESS

Published by Redemption Press, PO Box 427, Enumclaw, WA 98022.

Toll-Free (844) 2REDEEM (273-3336)

Redemption Press is honored to present this title in partnership with the author. The views expressed or implied in this work are those of the author. Redemption Press provides our imprint seal representing design excellence, creative content, and high-quality production.

Unless otherwise indicated, all Scripture quotations are taken from the Holy Bible, New Living Translation, copyright © 1996, 2004, 2015 by Tyndale House Foundation. Used by permission of Tyndale House Publishers, Inc., Carol Stream, Illinois 60188. All rights reserved.

ISBN: 978-1-64645-038-1 (Paperback)
978-1-64645-039-8 (ePub)
978-1-64645-040-4 (Mobi)

Library of Congress Catalog Card Number: 2020912591

I acknowledge and thank God for guiding me to write
this book. To Him be all the glory.

I also thank my dear friend Linda, who partnered with me
and encouraged me every step of the way.

Introduction

⌇⌇⌇ My Burden Is Light ⌇⌇⌇

For my yoke is easy to bear,
and the burden I give you is light.
Matthew 11:30

DO YOU EVER think, *Am I doing enough to serve God? Am I talented enough? Is the church the only place where I can serve? How can I serve God when I don't have time? I'm already overwhelmed with all my responsibilities and commitments!* Many of us grapple with these questions and concerns. We put a lot of pressure on ourselves. But those are our thoughts, not God's.

In the Bible, Jesus tells us His yoke is *easy.* We are the ones who make it harder than He intended. God's Word is full of stories about how God chose men and women before they were born and used them in unexpected ways to fulfill their purpose in His plan. God is doing the same with you, right where you are. This devotional will help you to see that He has an amazing plan that includes you, and He has placed you exactly where you need to be to play your part. With Christ, there is no guilt, no shame, and no condemnation (Rom. 8:1).

For years, I struggled with the same questions above. Between working full time and raising a family, there just wasn't enough time to serve God effectively, at least in the way *I thought* I needed to serve Him. Surely, I needed to be in some type of full-time Christian service to please God and "seriously" serve Him. I had a lot of guilt about this. I'd ask myself questions like, *Why am I wasting my life in this worldly job? Shouldn't I be doing something more for the kingdom?* I kept working, squeezing in as much ministry as I could. But it never seemed like enough. I still felt guilty, stressed, and exhausted.

Then I began to realize that God created me to serve Him in very different ways than I had thought. He chose where and when I was born, gave me specific talents and experiences that have shaped me into who I am today, and placed me in specific relational gardens so I could bloom for Him. He doesn't need me to be a missionary to another country. He doesn't need me to quit my job and go into full-time ministry. He can, and is, using me exactly where I am. I simply need to bloom where He has planted me! This insight has changed my life. It has eliminated so much stress and frustration, replacing the guilt with peace, joy, and satisfaction in serving God every day in all areas of my life. Now this doesn't mean God won't call you to be a missionary in Africa or to serve in full-time ministry—if He does, He has prepared this for you all along and you'll likely know it. But for most people, we are called to serve right where we are.

Not too long ago, God placed a desire in my heart to share this message with anyone who feels too busy to serve God as much as they would like to. Maybe you are like I was, serving in the church every week, and maybe at special activities, but still feeling like you're not doing enough— missing the fact that serving Him right where you are in your daily life is enough.

This book will take you on a thirty-day devotional journey to help you seek this truth. The message is twofold. The first section will focus on accepting who you are, showing you that God has orchestrated your birth and your life perfectly to grow you into the person you are today—a beautiful and unique flower in His marvelously planned garden. The second half focuses on the many different areas of your life where you can serve God every day—the various gardens you tend. Your gardens—home, work, social circles, church, and the world—are all ripe for planting and watering seeds of kindness, love, and faith. Opportunities abound for you to demonstrate and share your love and faith in Jesus in all areas of your life.

I pray God uses this devotional to help you see He has placed you perfectly in His well-planned garden of life. He is just waiting to see you bloom! Serving God has never been easier or more freeing once we take our expectations out of the equation and put aside the guilt. Jesus's yoke really is easy, His burden light. I'm excited for what you will discover.

Day 1

⤳ Uniquely You ⤝

For we are God's masterpiece. He has created
us anew in Christ Jesus, so we can do the good
things he planned for us long ago.
Ephesians 2:10

THERE ARE OVER 350,000 species of plants in this world. And even within the same species, each plant is unique. Have you ever looked at each rose in a garden? No two are the same. Each is different and beautiful in its own way. So are we. There is no one exactly like you. You are a unique blend of talents and experiences, with a life that is yours and yours alone. As it says in Ephesians 2:10, God has created each of us uniquely and placed us where we are to fulfill His plans.

I was born the youngest of eight children, and we lived in a rural, one-stoplight town in Pennsylvania. My graduating class was fewer than one hundred students. I was a small-town girl who loved my family and never dreamed of leaving my hometown. I expected to get married, work at a local company, and live out my life there. But in 1988, I moved out of my small town into a suburb of Cleveland, Ohio. And now, thirty years later, I am an executive at a large company, leading an organization of over six hundred people. Me, an executive? I never would have imagined that. I still have those small-town roots in me, but now I also have years of experiences that have shaped and changed me. God, the Master Gardener, had a plan for me since the beginning and has cultivated me into who I am today.

God also made you to be one of a kind. He made you just the way you are for a reason. You are not a mistake, a surprise, or a random accident. God chose to create you. He planted the seed of life in you. He chose when and where you'd be born. He is watering and caring for you to help you grow and bloom beautifully. There are times when the sun shines brightly and life is good. And, there are difficult times as well. I know it's like that in my own life.

Plants require pruning to grow to their fullest. The gardener cuts off the bad parts, and sometimes he even cuts off some of the good to let the rest bloom more fully. Like plants, we grow from both the good and difficult people and experiences in our lives. All of it comes together to make us into the people we are now.

To me, no other story in the Bible tells this better than Joseph's story. In the Old Testament, Joseph, son of Jacob, is a great example of a person who God perfectly created and developed to play an important role in His plan. Joseph's story, as told in Genesis chapters 37 and 39–45, is a strong example of God building up a person throughout their lifetime.

At the end of the story, Pharaoh made Joseph second in command over Egypt to prepare for and manage the food supply for a predicted famine. He had the right skills, the right heart, and the right position to make a significant difference for hundreds of thousands of people, ensuring that the food supply would last through the seven years of famine. How did he get to be the "perfect" person for the job? Was he simply born into it? Far from it. Joseph's story shows how a combination of being born at the right time, into the right family, and in the right place, as well as possessing God-given talents and a lifetime of experiences, all came together to do amazing things for God.

As we move through the following days, we'll follow Joseph's story, and you will learn more about how God has made you into the person you are today. I'll be sharing some of my own stories, and we'll spend more time thinking about how God shaped Joseph as well. I'm excited for you to grow in your understanding of how God has designed you to be uniquely you—how the timing and place of your birth, your talents, your personality, and your experiences have grown you into the incredible person you are right now.

Reflection

1. Take a few minutes to read about Joseph as he ruled in Egypt in Genesis 41:46–49, 53–57. How would you describe him? Then, take a few minutes to read about Joseph at the beginning of his story in Genesis 37:2–11. How would you describe him then?

_____

_____

_____

_____

_____

2. Think about who you were as a child and who you are now. How are you similar to the person you were in your past? How are you different?

_____

_____

_____

_____

_____

3. God loves you. You are His unique masterpiece. What are some of the things you most appreciate about yourself . . . things God created in you?

_____

_____

_____

_____

4. Is there anything God is saying to you today as you read and think about the lesson?

_____

_____

_____

_____

Today's Prayer

Dear Heavenly Father,

Thank You for creating me. Thank You for choosing just the right time and place for my birth and for giving me the experiences, both easy and hard, that have shaped me into the person I am today. Help me to appreciate the work You've done in me.

In Jesus's name I pray, Amen.

Day 2

⤳⤳ God's Perfect Timing ⤳⤳

You saw me before I was born. Every day of my
life was recorded in your book. Every moment
was laid out before a single day had passed.
Psalm 139:16

THERE IS A specific time for planting crops. You can't plant corn in the middle of the winter. You plant it in the spring, though you can't plant it too soon or the spring frost will kill it. You can't plant it too late, or it may miss the spring rains it needs to grow. Like planting a seed at just the right time causes the plant to prosper, grow, and thrive, God chose you to be born at the right time to grow you into the person you have become today and to use you to help His kingdom thrive. When we were born has a major impact on the person we are today.

I was born in 1961. Growing up, I rode my bike all over the neighborhood, played backyard games with my friends, and stayed outside until the streetlights came on. It was a time before electronic games and computers. We barely even watched TV. I wonder what it would have been like had I been born fifty years earlier. There would have been even less technology, and two major events in history would have been a part of my life—World War I and the Great Depression. I'm fortunate to have neither grown up in a time when millions of soldiers died defending our nation nor had to participate in bomb drills at school. I never had to ration food or go without it, as many did during the Great Depression. Both of these events would have had a profound impact on shaping my character and outlook on life. The reality is that hundreds of things would have been different had I been born in 1911, and I'd be a different person because of them.

The timing of when we are born has significance in God's plan. As God laid out His plan for all mankind's time on earth, He picked the precise time of every birth to optimize the effectiveness of His plan, which is to bring the maximum number of people into His eternal kingdom. Of all the people born throughout time, your birthdate denotes the exact and perfect time that God chose for you to join the human race and to become part of His plan. As it says in Psalm 139:16, every day, every moment of your life, has been carefully laid out by God, including the day you were born. Your birthdate was and is a special and precious day to God. It was your beginning, setting the stage for the rest of the story in the book of your life. The next time your birthday comes around, consider setting aside a time of worship to thank God for choosing the perfect day for your birth.

Reflection

1. There are so many things in your life that have been affected by when you were born. What are some key inventions or discoveries that have happened in your lifetime that have had an impact on your life?

---

2. What are some key world events that have happened in your lifetime that have had an impact on your life and your faith?

---

3. In what other ways has when you were born affected who you are today?

---

4. Is there anything God is saying to you today as you read and think about the lesson?

_____

_____

_____

_____

Today's Prayer

Dear Heavenly Father,

Thank You for choosing the perfect birthdate for me. Thank You that I was brought into this world on (fill in your birthdate). Thank You for the very life that You breathed into me that day and for every breath You've given me since then.

In Jesus's name I pray, Amen.

Day 3

❧ The Right Place for You ❧

Can papyrus reeds grow tall without a marsh?
Can marsh grass flourish without water?
Job 8:11

PLANTS ARE MEANT for specific environments. Each is designed to withstand the nature of its habitat. For example, a cactus does not need a lot of water and would drown in the rainforest. Oak trees need a lot of water and would die in the desert. Where you were planted (born) is a critical part of who you are, as your environment has been key to growing you into the person you are today.

I was born and raised in Union City, Pennsylvania. It is a small town founded in the 1800s. Redbrick buildings line the city streets. There were a number of businesses, the biggest being furniture factories, which made some of the best chairs in the country at the time. You could walk the streets at night with no fear; it was safe. As children, we weren't entertained by our parents. We found games to play on our own; kickball, red rover, and four square were some of my favorites. There were no fast-food joints, so we ate at home with our family around the table. It was a great environment to grow up in.

Being born in Union City has influenced my life in many ways. It instilled in me the importance of family and community. It helped me to be more innovative and creative, as we had to make up games to play. Its location had ripple effects on my life, like my choice of where to go to college. I visited Indiana University in Pennsylvania. The size was overwhelming. It had more students than the enitre population of my hometown! Instead, I chose to go to a small college where I was more comfortable. Even now, being from a small town has affected my life. As my husband and I contemplated where we wanted to live in retirement, my heart's desire was to move back to a small town with more of a country surrounding. In 2017, we moved from our overcrowded suburbs in Cleveland to Munson Township, a rural area of Ohio. I love it! I feel so much more at home here.

God decided long before you were born exactly *where* you would be born. He chose your country, state, hometown, and neighborhood. Where you started life was exactly where God wanted you to sprout forth. The type of place where you grew up—whether inner-city, suburbs, or the country—played an important role in shaping your thoughts, values, and character. God also may have moved you around, placing you in multiple environments during your life, all of which have molded and shaped you further.

You, of course, have influenced every place you have been as well. God has used you throughout your life to impact people in each location you've lived. You have touched many throughout your life, sometimes in big ways, sometimes in small ways. God uses you in ways you know and see and in so many ways that you don't. God knew just where to plant you and when to transplant you, leading you to where you are now.

Reflection

1. Think about where you were born and raised. What are some aspects of your birthplace that you remember the most?

_____

_____

_____

_____

_____

2. Where we are born has a profound impact on our path in life. What significant decisions have you made in your life that were impacted by where you grew up?

_____

_____

_____

_____

_____

3. It's amazing to think about how where we were born and raised has influenced us throughout our lives—even up to this very moment. How has your birthplace affected who you are today?

_____

_____

_____

_____

4. Is there anything God is saying to you today as you read and think about the lesson?

_____

_____

_____

_____

Today's Prayer

Dear God,

Thank You for my hometown and my neighborhood. Whether I consider it good or bad, You chose it for me. Being born in (fill in your town) has had a significant impact on who I am, and that has always been a part of Your plan. Help me to better understand and appreciate how it has influenced the person I am today.

In Jesus's name I pray, Amen.

Day 4

⤜⤜⤜ Joseph–Perfectly Planted ⤜⤜⤜

So Jacob settled again in the land of Canaan,
where his father had lived as a foreigner.
Genesis 37:1

GETTING A PLANT to bloom takes a lot of planning. You must prepare the seed, choose the right soil, bury it at the right depth, and put it in the best place to get just the right amount of sun and rain. God takes this same care when planning each person's life, just as He did with Joseph's life. Joseph was born and raised in the land of Canaan into a family of sheepherders. He was the eleventh born of the twelve sons of Jacob. His life took several twists and turns that affected his life and those around him in significant ways.

Joseph was Jacob's favorite son. Why was he the favorite? The Bible is not entirely clear on this, but let's consider what it does say. Genesis 37:3 says, "Jacob loved Joseph more than any of his other children because Joseph had been born to him in his old age." It seems that Joseph may have been one of those "surprise" children. That surely endeared him to Jacob. Also, Joseph's mother was Rachel, who was Jacob's true love. Rachel had only two of Jacob's twelve sons—the last two—and she died giving birth to Benjamin. Those factors—having Joseph in his old age, loving Rachel, and then losing her—must have caused Jacob to have a great love for Joseph. Unfortunately, this great love led to great jealousy among his brothers. Over time, as his brothers saw that their father loved Joseph more, they grew to hate him and decided to get rid of him.

Timing and location now play a key part in the story. His brothers initially plotted to kill Joseph. However, at just the right time, a caravan of Ishmaelite traders passed by, and the brothers decided to sell him instead. The Ishmaelites were on their way to Egypt. We know that at the end of the story, God needed Joseph in Egypt. Had he been raised elsewhere, even if the other facts of the story were the same, he would not have ended up in Egypt. Where he was born was a significant factor in his life and ultimately in the lives of the hundreds of thousands of people he saved from the famine.

Like many of us, I would guess that Joseph did not give much thought to where or when he was born. He likely had no idea that both would be so important to lead him on a journey he never imagined. God had great plans in store for Joseph, and for them to play out, God chose the perfect time and place for his birth. God has done the same for each of us! The combination of when we were born, where we were born, and the places we've traveled in life's journey, puts us in the right place at the right time to do incredible things for God.

Most of us will likely never have the impact that Joseph had, but we do have an impact on every person who God brings into our lives. Chances are that there are multiple examples of how your influence on people has changed them or altered their course in some way. It all gets back to how each of us, and the journey we take, intersects with others according to His will and plans. You can see it in Joseph's life, and if you reflect on your life, I'm sure you'll find examples there too.

Reflection

1. God's perfect placement of Joseph in Canaan eventually led him to Egypt, where he would one day be second-in-command. Describe the path from where you were born to where you are now.

_____

_____

_____

_____

2. As you reflect on your life's journey, describe a situation where you were in the right place at the right time to have a positive impact on someone's life.

_____

_____

_____

_____

3. Joseph's life took a crazy turn when he was sold to the Ishmaelites, which changed the course of his life. Describe a situation in your life that changed your direction, and consider how where you were at the time played a key part.

_____

_____

_____

_____

4. Is there anything God is saying to you today as you read and think about the lesson?

_____

_____

_____

_____

Today's Prayer

Dear Heavenly Father,

Your plans for our lives are so complex and so perfect. I cannot possibly fully understand them. However, please let me understand more and see glimpses. Help me to appreciate the timing and place of my birth and how it has affected me and the lives of others. Help me to fully trust in You and the good things You have planned for me.

In Jesus's name I pray, Amen.

Day 5

⤜⤜⤜ Tailor-Made ⤛⤛⤛

---

*You made all the delicate, inner parts of my body
and knit me together in my mother's womb.*
Psalm 139:13

A S GOD KNIT you together in your mother's womb, He chose
what kind of person you would be. He gave you your
personality—the combination of characteristics or quali-
ties forming your distinctive character. Think of your personality like a plant. Are you a giant, colorful sunflower,
radiant and outgoing? Maybe you are more like a mighty,
sturdy oak tree, strong and confident. Or, perhaps you are
more delicate, like a small and lovely violet. Whatever your
personality, the most important thing to remember is that
God chose it for you, and it has a purpose!

I think my personality is like a coconut. The outside
of a coconut is tough and hard to break, and I am like
that in some ways. I am assertive. I stand up for what I
believe. I am a person who likes to be in charge. But when
you break a coconut open, you find a softer interior, and

like the coconut, I am sensitive on the inside. I care deeply about others. My feelings are easily hurt. I cry over sad movies, commercials, and even just because I see someone else crying!

Your personality is a big part of who you are. It has a significant influence on everything you do. My personality shaped me well for my role at work, creating an ideal balance. Together, my assertiveness and how I care for the people I lead makes me an effective leader. At times, my "take charge" nature is needed in situations God puts me in, and at other times, my sensitivity is what He needs. He uses both aspects of my personality in many ways.

Your personality is not something you decide upon or learn. God chose what your personality would be before you were even born. I've seen this in my grandchildren. You can see their personalities at a very young age. Some are outgoing, thriving on activity and always wanting to be "on stage." Others are more introspective and like to play one-on-one. Some are more imaginative and like to think outside the box, while others are more black-and-white in their thinking and get upset when the rules are not followed. Each child is different, and their personalities affect their lives and those around them.

God chose your personality and made you the way you are for a specific purpose. An outgoing sunflower can bring fun and joy to those who need cheering up, while a quiet and delicate violet can come alongside someone who is hurting and needs a shoulder to cry on. God needs all kinds of people. We each have a unique personality that is an important part of the well-planned garden that God has put together to carry out His work.

Reflection

1. Take a few minutes to think about your personality. What aspects of your attitude and behavior have always been a part of who you are? As you consider this, what kind of plant would you liken yourself to?

_____

_____

_____

_____

2. How is your personality a benefit to those around you?

_____

_____

_____

_____

3. Think about someone you are close to who has a very different personality than you. How have you benefited from their personality?

_____

_____

_____

_____

4. Is there anything God is saying to you today as you read and think about the lesson?

_____

_____

_____

_____

_____

_____

Today's Prayer

Dear God,

Thank You for how You have made me. Thank You for my personality—my (fill in with your traits). It is wonderful how all the different personality traits You have given me and those around me blend to create a magnificent garden of people helping each other in unique ways. Please help me to use my personality as You intended.

In Jesus's name I pray, Amen.

Day 6

❧ You've Got Talent! ❧

---

*The human body has many parts, but the many
parts make up one whole body.
So it is with the body of Christ.*
1 Corinthians 12:12

PLANTS SERVE MANY purposes. Fruits and vegetables provide delicious nutrition, and there are so many varieties. Did you know there are over 1,600 species of bananas? And that's just bananas! Trees provide the very oxygen we need to live, materials for our homes, and shade for a hot summer day. Flowers smell amazing, provide pollen for bees to make their honey, and brighten the day of those who receive them. All plants have multiple purposes, just like we do. God has given us each a different set of talents, which enables hundreds of things to be accomplished. I've got talents, and so do you!

I've always been good at organizing and planning, from organizing my closet or my day to planning a simple event or a two-week cross-country vacation. These God-given talents have also shaped my career and placed me in the position and company where I work. This has, in turn, brought me into the lives of hundreds of people I otherwise would have never met, all because I have the talents of planning and organizing.

God's design for your life includes the talents He has given you. Each of us has a unique set of talents. The talents He has given you have put you in many different circumstances. They've taken you down certain paths in your personal and work life, bringing you into contact with the people He intended you to meet.

Do you ever look at a musician and wish you could sing like they do? Or cook like your sister can? Or teach like your friend? The list goes on and on. Try not to be envious; if you can't sing, it's because God didn't choose you to have that talent. When you appreciate others' talents, be sure to appreciate your own too. First Corinthians 12:15–18 says,

> If the foot says, "I am not a part of the body because I am not a hand," that does not make it any less a part of the body. If the ear says, "I am not part of the body because I am not an eye," would that make it any less a part of the body? If the whole body were an eye, how would you hear? Or if your whole body were an ear, how would you smell anything? But our bodies have many parts, and God has put each part just where He wants it.

God made you just as you are, and you contribute to

this world in your own unique way. Each of us plays an equally important part in God's plan. Your talents will impact a person, who inspires two more, who each shape the lives of three others, and so on. For example, let's say that God has given you musical talent, and you sing a song during a morning worship set at church that deeply touches a person in the audience. It gives them the hope and guidance they need for a situation in their life. They then handle a situation differently than they would have, and their entire family is impacted by their actions. Before you know it, using your talent—no matter what it is—has affected many people. God multiplies the influence you have when you simply use the talents He has blessed you with! Never underestimate the power of the talents God has given you and how He will use them.

Reflection

1. List at least three of your talents. Your talents likely coincide with things you love to do.

_____

_____

_____

_____

_____

_____

2. How have these talents affected your path in life? What are things you have done in your life because of your talents?

_____

_____

_____

_____

3. How have these talents affected the people in your life? Consider the influence you've had on people you would have never met had it not been for your talents.

_____

_____

_____

_____

4. Is there anything God is saying to you today as you read and think about the lesson?

_____

_____

_____

_____

Today's Prayer

Dear Heavenly Father,

Thank you, Lord, for the talents You have given me. Thank You for (insert each one you wrote above). Help me to be grateful for my talents and not be envious of the talents of others. It is amazing to think about all the people I have met and influenced because of the talents You have given me. Thank you for each and every one of them.

In Jesus's name I pray, Amen.

Day 7

⤳⤳ Joseph, the Dreamer ⤳⤳

---

*The LORD was with Joseph, so he succeeded in
everything he did as he served in the home of
his Egyptian master. Potiphar noticed this and
realized that the LORD was with Joseph, giving
him success in everything he did. This pleased
Potiphar, so he soon made Joseph his personal
attendant. He put him in charge of his entire
household and everything he owned.*
Genesis 39:2–4

NOTHING GROWS WITHOUT God. He provides the soil, sun, and
rain that every plant needs to bloom. He is the Creator
of all life, and the earth He created is teeming with beautiful plants of all kinds. I love the beauty of a sunflower.
It starts so small and grows so tall, and it almost seems
to be smiling as it blooms with bright yellow petals. The
same is true for us. God provides everything we need to
bloom fully for Him. Like us, Joseph's personality and talents played out perfectly in God's purpose for his life. He
had many talents, like interpreting dreams, administration

skills, and the ability to lead. These were exactly the talents Joseph needed to accomplish God's plan to save His people.

When Joseph was at home with his brothers, he began having dreams. These weren't just any dreams; they were prophecies of the future. In Genesis 37:6–7, Joseph said to his brothers, "Listen to this dream. We were out in the field, tying up bundles of grain. Suddenly my bundle stood up, and your bundles gathered around and bowed low before mine!" Joseph was excited about his dream. His brothers, however, did not share in his excitement. Instead, they became angry because Joseph's dreams put him above them, making him out to be more important—just like he was with their father. They did not stop to consider whether the dream was from God or whether his dream could be prophetic. In verse 8 it says, "And they hated him all the more because of his dream and the way he talked about them."

Think about what this says about Joseph's personality. Did he know that his brothers hated him and that telling them about the dream would make them even more upset? Did he share it simply to stoke their anger? Did he love being the favorite son and want to show off his superiority by sharing the dreams? It's not entirely clear, but I don't think that fits the Joseph you read about as you continue with his story. I think he may have been truly excited about this interesting dream he had and just wanted to share it with his brothers. It's possible, however, that he was prideful. As I think about the journey God took him on, it certainly humbled him.

When Joseph arrived in Egypt, God gave him great success in everything he did. Scripture says God was "with Joseph" and that was why he prospered (Gen. 39:2). When his master, Potiphar, saw this, he put Joseph in charge of his entire household, entrusting everything he owned to him. God gave Joseph various talents to take on such a large responsibility—including skills in leadership, organization, and relationship building. Later, when Joseph ended up in prison, he was put in charge of all those held there, yet another testament to what must have been truly remarkable natural leadership.

The personality and talents you have been given are from God. It did not say that Joseph was successful because of his talents. It says he was successful because "the LORD was with him." It's important that we don't look at ourselves as the source of our successes; otherwise, we begin to rely on ourselves instead of God. We can begin to trust too much in what we can accomplish and not enough on what God can accomplish through us. Always give glory to God for the successes in your life, even those you helped make happen. Remember that He is the source of your talents and skills.

Reflection

1. Take some time to read through the story of Joseph (Gen. 37:1–28, 39). What talents or personality traits do you think Joseph had?

_____

_____

_____

_____

2. Think of some of your greatest successes. What talents did God give you that blossomed in these situations?

_____

_____

_____

_____

3. What is a good way to ensure that you always remember and acknowledge that God gave you your skills and is the source of your success?

_____

_____

_____

_____

4. Is there anything God is saying to you today as you read and think about the lesson?

_____

_____

_____

_____

_____

_____

Today's Prayer

Dear Heavenly Father,

Thank you, God, for the successes in my life. Thank You for being the true source of those successes. I cannot do anything without You and without the life, talents, and skills You've given me. Help me to always remember to thank You and praise You for any successes I experience.

In Jesus's name I pray, Amen.

Day 8

⤳ Tenderly Cared For ⤳

---

*And I am certain that God, who began
the good work within you, will continue his
work until it is finally finished on the day
when Christ Jesus returns.*
Philippians 1:6

ONCE PLANTED, A seed requires nourishment and protection to grow into the plant it is meant to be. For plants to grow, they must receive the right amount of sun and rain. Consider an oak tree. It starts as a teeny, tiny acorn, no bigger than a quarter. As the earth and water nourish it, it first sprouts into a small green plant. Over time, the roots grow deeper, the trunk grows wider and taller, and it becomes a giant, magnificent tree, towering one-hundred-feet tall over its surroundings. From a small acorn to a marvel of nature, it's really quite incredible!

Just like plants, we also need nourishment and care to grow and fully become the people God wants us to be. God nourishes us in many ways. His Word is water for our souls. He draws us closer in prayer. He also nurtures us, using the people and events—good or bad—that He brings into our lives.

One of the strongest influences in my life was my mother. She has had a significant effect on who I am today. She was an extremely generous person, always sharing everything she had. She wasn't rich, but she often "loaned" money to her grandchildren, knowing she would never get it back. It didn't matter to her. They had a need and she could help, so she did. My mom bought presents for everyone in the family, including the child of her grandson's girlfriend. I believe at her last Christmas she bought gifts for over seventy people! She loved doing it.

I love giving too. It brings me great joy to give gifts to others. I love picking out just the right gifts and seeing them bring a smile to the faces of the receivers. My mom also loved spending time with her grandchildren, and there was often one or more of them at her house any time you went to visit. This was the norm, and it influenced me to want to spend a lot of time with my grandchildren as well. These are just two of the many ways she influenced me.

Just as a gardener tends to his garden, so God tends to you through the people He places in your life. Sometimes their habits become yours. The way you view the world is greatly influenced by the perspectives of the people closest to you. While I love spending time with my grandchildren because of my mother's influence, my husband saw very little interaction between his mother and her grandchildren. So though he loves them as much as I do, he doesn't want to spend nearly as much time with them. Neither is right or wrong; we were just influenced differently. God uses those differences to balance us out—we see the grandchildren a lot, but not so much that we wear out our welcome!

God has watered and nurtured you through your experiences with various people. The things they taught you and the example they set with their life, whether positive or negative, played a part in who you are today. There may have been some people who felt like warm sunshine beaming into your life, influencing you in positive ways. There may have been others who felt like a thunderstorm! They all have affected you. You are a culmination of God working through the people in your life. He makes use of everything and everyone in your life to help you learn, grow, and become a better person who is more equipped to serve Him wherever He has planted you.

Reflection

1. Who has been a "ray of sunshine" and had a positive influence on your life? How have they helped shape who you are today?

_____

_____

_____

_____

_____

_____

2. Who is someone in your life that felt more like a thunderstorm, and how did you grow or learn from that?

_____

_____

_____

_____

3. Whose sunshine have you been? Who is someone you have greatly influenced in a positive way, and how has it affected who they are today?

_____

_____

_____

_____

4. Is there anything God is saying to you today as you read and think about the lesson?

_____

_____

_____

_____

_____

_____

Bloom!

Today's Prayer

Dear Heavenly Father,

Thank You for the people You have placed in my life—those who are like sunshine and those who are like storms. I realize that You can and have used both types of people to help me grow. I thank You for how you've used me to help others grow too. Help me to be sunshine in the lives of those I touch.

In Jesus's name I pray, Amen.

Day 9

Joseph's Journey

So it was God who sent me here, not you!
And he is the one who made me an adviser to
Pharaoh—the manager of his entire palace and
the governor of all Egypt.
Genesis 45:8

THE PEOPLE AND events in Joseph's life had a significant impact on him. So far, we've already touched on how his father's great love and his brothers' jealousy resulted in him being sold into slavery. That took him to Egypt and the house of Potiphar. This gave him a position of great power, which was then stripped away when Potiphar's wife lied about Joseph making advances on her. He landed in prison, where he again rose to leadership.

In the next part of the story, the cupbearer and the baker of the Pharaoh did something that put them in prison as well, and the captain of the guard assigned them to Joseph. A connection was made. They both had dreams, and Joseph, through God, interpreted the meanings. Then, what he told them, happened. The cupbearer returned to the service of the Pharaoh, and eventually the Pharaoh had a dream that no one could interpret. The cupbearer remembered what Joseph did, and he was called in to interpret the Pharaoh's dream. The interpretation of the dream was that famine was coming to the land, and someone needed to help the nation prepare for it. The Pharaoh chose Joseph.

Wow! That's a lot of crazy circumstances that caused Joseph to be second-in-command over all of Egypt. His preparation for the famine saved hundreds of thousands of people, including his own family. I'm amazed when I consider how many players and circumstances were needed to get Joseph to this exact place at the right time. Many of the circumstances did not seem particularly good at the time (sold by his brothers, imprisoned under false charges, initially forgotten by the cupbearer). However, God used all of them to bring Joseph to his crowning accomplishment in saving Egypt's people, and his own, from the famine. Remarkable!

Most of us probably won't do something quite as big as saving hundreds of thousands of people from death. However, you have important work to do that will contribute to God's children being saved from spiritual death. He has prepared you for that work. He needs you. No matter how small or large your part, join God to save as many as possible for Him and His kingdom.

Reflection

1.   Take a minute and write a list of all the people who influenced Joseph's journey to become second-in-command

of Egypt. Pick one or two of them and describe how they influenced his life.

_____

_____

_____

_____

2. Reflect on God's working in your own life. What are some of the key events that altered your path and led you to where you are in life today?

_____

_____

_____

_____

3. Like Joseph, have you had some dark periods in your life that were necessary for you to end up where you are today?

_____

_____

_____

_____

_____

4. Is there anything God is saying to you today as you read and think about the lesson?

_____

_____

_____

_____

_____

_____

Today's Prayer

Dear God,

The story of Joseph is such a good illustration of how You use everything in our lives—the good, the bad, and the ugly—to shape us into who we are today. Help us to appreciate how each circumstance has changed us or led us to different places in our lives. Thank You for who I am today as a result of all the things that have happened up to this point.

In Jesus's name I pray, Amen.

Day 10

❧ The Full Bouquet ❧

---

*Each of you should continue to live in whatever
situation the LORD has placed you, and remain
as you were when God first called you.
This is my rule for all the churches.*
1 Corinthians 7:17

YOU HAVE SPENT the past few days discovering that you are
God's masterpiece—a work of art He has been working
on since the day you were conceived. He chose when and
where you would be born, gave you your personality and
natural talents, and placed many people in your life to influence you. As you consider who you are right at this moment, know that God has been working behind the scenes
all the time to shape you into the person He needs to work
a special part of His plan.

God uses a variety of people, spread all over the world,
to achieve His goals. He doesn't need everyone to be a missionary, a pastor, a ministry leader, or a full-time ministry worker. He needs most of us to be ministering to the

people we interact with during our day-to-day lives. He needs you, soccer mom, to reach the kids and parents on your kid's team who never go to church. He needs you, awesome friend, to come alongside and comfort someone who is hurting. He needs you, businesswoman, to treat your coworkers according to your Christian values so that you can be an example for others. He needs you, sister, to show the love of Jesus to that sibling you have a difficult relationship with. He needs us to serve Him where He has placed us—to bloom where we are planted!

Who we are—the total package—is important. Here's how I would describe myself today: I am a wife, mother, grandmother, sibling, daughter, aunt, coworker, boss, and friend. I am assertive, sensitive, kind, respectful, impatient, and generous. I am a procrastinator, a leader, a hard worker, and a great planner. Sometimes I can be outgoing, but I like my quiet time too. In my spare time, I like doing things with my family and watching science-fiction shows and movies with my husband. I like to travel to national and state parks and the beach because I love nature and enjoy exploring the beautiful land that God has created. My husband, father, sisters, brothers, children, and other family members are my true circle of friends, along with one other dear friend, Linda. This is me, and every aspect I've just described is what it is because it is what God has chosen for me.

You are an amazing woman, one who God has been crafting for many years. You are a masterpiece in His eyes, and He's not done yet. He will continue to build us and change us and grow us into even more beautiful bouquets that will bless others. God wants to use the person we are today to tend the people in the gardens of our lives. All we have to do is say, "Yes, Lord, I'm ready to serve you where you've planted me!"

Reflection

1. It's amazing to think about the "whole package" that is you! Like I did above, make a list describing yourself.

_____

_____

_____

_____

_____

2. As you reflect on all the things we've covered—when and where you were born, your talents and personality, and your life experiences—what is something about who you are today that all of them played a part in creating?

_____

_____

_____

_____

_____

3. What is God doing in your life this very moment that is changing you?

_____

_____

_____

_____

4. Is there anything God is saying to you today as you read and think about the lesson?

_____

_____

_____

_____

Today's Prayer

Dear Heavenly Father,

It is truly amazing to think about how You have been at work in my life since the very beginning. Thank You for all that You've done within me and around me to shape me into the person I am today. Help me to see and appreciate the many ways in which You are still working in my life. I love You, Lord, and am ready to better understand how You want me to serve You where I am and through who I am.

In Jesus's name I pray, Amen.

Day 11

~~~ Where Are Your Gardens? ~~~

But you will receive power when the
Holy Spirit comes upon you.
And you will be my witnesses, telling people
about me everywhere—in Jerusalem, throughout
Judea, in Samaria, and to the ends of the earth.

Acts 1:8

GOD HAS PLANTED you in different gardens. In some, you may be like a flower in a small window box, like at home. In others you may be like a flower in a field of clover, one of hundreds, such as at your workplace. In all cases, God wants to use you. As a disciple of Jesus, you have an opportunity to witness in many different ways to people all around you. We will explore each of these different gardens where you can have an impact. For today, I'd just like you to take a few minutes to think about the gardens you are in.

In Acts 1:8, Jesus gives His disciples a mission for their lives. This verse describes witnessing in their backyard (Jerusalem), their neighboring communities (Judea and Samaria), and the entire world ("the ends of the earth").

We are missionaries in the same way: serving God close to home, expanding to our local area, and then reaching out to other countries around the world.

We all have an opportunity to serve God in our homes and family. This is your Jerusalem, your backyard. This is a garden you live in, and the people you interact with every day. While it's the one you are in the most, it's often the hardest garden to witness and serve in.

Next, is your community garden—your Judea and Samaria. You don't just belong to one community; you belong to many. This includes social circles such as sports, clubs, friendships, and your neighborhood. It includes your church and your workplace, two gardens that are likely to be vastly different from each other when it comes to the type of people involved and the work to be done.

Your last garden is the world, where you are to be a witness to the ends of the earth. Before you book your round-the-world trip, know that this is a garden you can cultivate without ever leaving the comfort of your home.

God has planted you in many different gardens, and each is a mission field. It's important that you understand and think about what these are in your life. Only then can you see the opportunities each garden gives you and begin to serve God by blooming in each one.

Reflection

Take some time and think about the many gardens you are in—the places and groups you are a part of, the church you go to, the relationships you are in, the job you have, and so forth.

1. First, let's think about Jerusalem—your home and family. Describe the different family groups you are a part of.

_____

_____

_____

_____

_____

_____

2. Moving on to Judea and Samaria, list out the different community groups you are part of. Think about the various things you do regularly. This can be obvious things, like your job and church. Think, too, about groups of people you see regularly—could be the other parents of your kid's baseball team or your golf buddies. There may be a few or a lot of these. Either is fine!

_____

_____

_____

_____

_____

_____

3. Which of these gardens do you spend the most time in? What is your role in that garden? Who do you influence and how?

_____

_____

_____

_____

_____

4. Is there anything God is saying especially to you today as you read and think about this lesson?

_____

_____

_____

_____

_____

Today's Prayer

Dear God,

Thank You for the many gardens You have planted me in. I ask that You would bring to mind any I have not considered and add them to my list. I want to understand each of the gardens of my life so that I can consider how my being in them may fit into Your plan.

In Jesus's name I pray, Amen.

Day 12

❧ Aligning to God's Will ❧

For the word of God is alive and powerful.
It is sharper than the sharpest two-edged sword,
cutting between soul and spirit, between joint
and marrow. It exposes our innermost thoughts
and desires.
Hebrews 4:12

HAVE YOU EVER cared for a plant that would simply not respond? You tried watering it just right, putting it in the sunshine, and fertilizing it, but nothing seemed to work. The plant would not grow. Just like that plant, there may be gardens you are in where your efforts to witness or serve God don't appear to be having any effect. Try as you might to make a difference, there's just no growth or fruit. On the other hand, there also may be plants in a garden somewhere that are starving for attention and are just waiting for you to join them, places where God wants you to help others on their journey towards Him.

Yesterday you thought about all the gardens you are in. We will dive into how you can serve God in different ways in each of them, but before we do that, let's first consider if you are in the gardens that God wants you to be in. Are you in the places God wants you to be? Are you in the job He wants you to be in? Are you in the clubs or other social groups He desires for you? Are there other new gardens He'd like you to join? How do you know? Discerning God's will is an important part of being a Christian. There are lots of books written on this topic, so I won't go in-depth. However, let me share a few simple things over the next few days that may help you, and then we will circle back to how this applies to your gardens.

An important way to discern the will of God is to read the Word of God. God's will is in God's Word. The Bible is full of verses telling us how to live. Many refer to the Bible as the "instruction manual for life." So often we search for God's will about something, and He has already given us the answer in the Bible. For example, let's say you are being offered a new job that comes with a much higher income. You'll be able to buy that newer, bigger house and better car, but you'll have to give up a lot of family time, as the new job will be very demanding. If your sole motivation for taking the job is to pursue more "stuff," you should consider this verse in God's Word that describes His will for us:

> Don't store up treasures here on earth, where moths eat them and rust destroys them, and where thieves break in and steal. Store your treasures in heaven, where moths and rust cannot destroy, and thieves do not break in and steal. Wherever your treasure is, there the desires of your heart will also be. (Matt. 6:19–21)

Applying this verse to the situation helps you to see that spending time accumulating more stuff should not be your focus; rather, spending time investing in your family and your relationships will last forever.

Wondering what God wants you to do about that person in your life who you'd call an enemy? The answer is clear in this verse: "But I say, love your enemies! Pray for those who persecute you!" (Matt. 5:44). Is there someone in your life who comes to mind as you read this verse? Perhaps someone who is difficult to work with or challenging to be with? Instead of focusing on what you don't like about them, which can cause bitterness, Jesus says you should love them and pray for them. I encourage you to read Matthew 5:43–48 to get the full context of this command.

As you seek God's will, look to what He says in the Bible. It's not just a book; it's not just words. As it says in Hebrews 4:12, God's Word "is alive and powerful." It has the power to change you, and it has the wisdom you need to know the will of God for your life.

Reflection

1. Take some time to read your Bible today, and find three verses that describe how God wants you to live. From what you've read, write down things He wants you to do or things He wants you to stop doing.

---

2. Think about the decisions you have on your mind right now. Are there any that God's Word has already answered for you?

_____

_____

_____

_____

3. Consider that Jesus told us to love our neighbors and our enemies. Is there someone in your life right now who makes this difficult for you? Take a minute and write down three positive things about that person. And then add them to your prayer list!

_____

_____

_____

_____

4. Is there anything God is saying especially to you today as you read and think about this lesson?

_____

_____

_____

_____

Today's Prayer

Dear God,

Thank You for Your Word. It is rich with wisdom and advice for my life. I will seek Your will for my life by reading the Bible regularly. When I'm faced with challenges and decisions in my life, please guide me to the answers within it. Help me to be more loving to the difficult people in my life. I pray for (fill in the name of your challenging person from question three). I pray that You will bless them and help them in whatever way they need today. Please give me more patience and help me to love them.

In Jesus's name I pray, Amen.

Day 13

⤳ Daily Surrender ⤳

May your Kingdom come soon.
May your will be done on earth,
as it is in heaven.
Matthew 6:10

Bonsai is a Japanese art form that produces small plants that mimic full-sized trees. The artist controls the size of the plant by keeping it in a small pot and pruning its roots. They also carefully snip branches and leaves to get it to grow into a beautiful mini tree.

We are created in the image of God, and it is His will to make us more like Jesus. We are like that mini tree, a copy of the likeness of the big tree, God. He is the artist working on making us look more like Him and guiding you to the life He has planned for you. However, we often want to be in control and do things on our own. We like to go down the paths we choose instead of the ones God has in mind for us, and our branches tend to grow out of control. If you truly want what God wants for your life, you have to surrender your own will and let Him lead you. This is not a one-and-done thing, as we will constantly battle our human nature to do things according to our own desires. Therefore, you need to surrender to God's will *every day.*

One way to do this is to pray each morning, submitting to your heavenly Father's will. Simply pray something like this:

> Dear Heavenly Father, I surrender my will to you today. I pray that you will guide my thoughts, my words, and my actions so they are aligned to your will. I pray that I will not miss any opportunity you have planned for me this day. Help me to see and act upon them according to your will.

It makes sense to allow the almighty God, who can see into the future, to guide your life. However, surrendering to God in all things is hard! Some things may be easier to surrender to Him than others. Perhaps submitting to His will in your parenting is easy. However, it may be more challenging in your marriage, your finances, or how you spend your free time.

Every day is full of many decisions and activities. While I try to submit and be sensitive to God's will, my own desires often rise to the surface and take over. For example, at Christmas in 2018, my husband and I were living in a tiny place while our new home was being built. Therefore, hosting Christmas at my place was not an option, so the plan was to meet at my daughter's home. But I had a strong, selfish desire to host Christmas, so I rented a place for the weekend—without talking to God or my daughter. How I treated her was not according to God's will. My daughter, God bless her, extended grace to me, and in the end, we came up with a revised plan that worked well for everyone.

Praying each morning, surrendering your will, and letting God guide your thoughts, words, and actions are great ways to ensure you are following His will for your life. It's also very freeing. He knows all things and how every one of your decisions will turn out. He knows what is best for you. He wants what is best for you. Putting Him in control of your life is the best decision you'll ever make.

Reflection

1. What areas of your life do you find easy to surrender to God's will?

_____

_____

_____

_____

2. As you think about surrendering to God's will every day, what areas of your life are hard to relinquish? Why is that?

_____

_____

_____

_____

3. Write out your own version of the daily surrender prayer on a separate piece of paper and put it where you will remember to pray it each day. Commit to doing this daily.

_____

_____

_____

_____

4. Is there anything God is saying especially to you today as you read and think about this lesson?

_____

_____

_____

_____

Today's Prayer

Dear Mighty God,

You have infinite knowledge and power. I know that I can tap into both by aligning with and following Your will. You know what is best for my life. I surrender my will to You and ask You to guide all areas of my life. Please reveal to me the areas where I am not letting You lead, and help me to release them to You. I want Your will to be done today and always.

In Jesus's name I pray, Amen.

Day 14

❧ Ask and Listen ☙

If you need wisdom, ask our generous God,
and he will give it to you.
He will not rebuke you for asking.
James 1:5

The sun gives life to plants, and they know it. They reach for the sun. I've seen flowers turn their heads toward the morning sun and then face the other direction come afternoon. They know that the energy they draw from the sun keeps them alive, and they want to absorb as much as they can throughout the day. The same is true for us and our connection to God through prayer. Prayer is a source of life for us. We draw energy and life from God when we pray to Him. Prayer is also a key way to seek and know God's will.

When you want to know a fact about something, you just "ask Google." When you want to know God's will about something, just "ask God"! As it says in James 1:5, God is a generous God and wants to help you. He's waiting for you to pray and seek wisdom from Him. The Lord knows every decision you need to make, the path each choice will take you down, and how each will turn out. Wisdom from the Almighty is the best advice you can receive.

So, when you pray and ask God for guidance, how do you hear His answer? Here are a couple of things that have been true in my prayer life. When I pray, at times I get an immediate answer from the Holy Spirit—an answer that just comes into my thoughts. God will speak to you in this way. Be careful though, that your own desires and thoughts don't drown God's out. If God's answer is always aligned to your desires every time you ask Him something in prayer, you probably are not hearing Him clearly.

A second way God speaks to me in prayer is by using my emotions. When I'm trying to make a choice, I'll often find that one way feels right, while the other does not. The wrong decision will actually make my stomach hurt when I ask about it in prayer.

Another way God may reveal His will to you can be learned from the story of Balaam and his donkey in Numbers 22:21–41. The Lord was trying to stop Balaam from going on his journey, and Balaam's donkey, seeing the Angel of the Lord, stopped several times, preventing Balaam from going further. Balaam kept trying to get the donkey to move so he could continue on his journey. When the Lord finally revealed Himself to Balaam, he said, "Look, I have come to block your way because you are stubbornly resisting me." God was trying to get Balaam's attention so that He could redirect his path.

Through prayer, I invite God to redirect me. I will pray to God that He would put a "donkey in the road," something that will stop me if what I am doing is not aligned to His will. He has answered this prayer on more than one occasion. One time, this happened when I was planning to visit my son and his family. I was lying in bed the night before the trip and felt drawn to ask God to "put the donkey in the road" if I was not to go. The next morning, I woke up with a significant case of vertigo. I couldn't get out of bed, let alone drive. While I was disappointed to cancel my trip, I trust that there was a very good reason God didn't want me to go, and I'm grateful He prevented it from happening.

Prayer is powerful. It connects you to God. Talking to God through prayer is needed to have a good relationship with Him. He wants to talk with you. He wants to answer your questions and help guide you.

Talk to God about the gardens you are in. Ask Him if there are any that He'd like you to leave. Do you have a garden that gives you one problem after another, and nothing seems to go right? If so, it may be that God doesn't want you to be there. Ask Him if there are new gardens He wants you to enter. Pray, ask, and listen for His response.

Reflection

1. How is your prayer life? If it's not what you want it to be, what is one new prayer habit you can start today?

_____

_____

_____

_____

2. Are there gardens you are in where you've run into many obstacles? This could be a specific relationship or group where keeping it going is difficult at every turn. Pray and ask God if He is trying to get you to move out of that garden.

_____

_____

_____

_____

_____

_____

3. Are there new gardens you are about to enter? Perhaps a new group you are about to join or a new job? List any new ones here and prayerfully consider whether they are aligned to God's will. Pray for God to "send a donkey" to stop you if any of them are not the right path for you.

_____

_____

_____

_____

_____

_____

4. Is there anything God is saying especially to you today as you read and think about this lesson?

_____

_____

_____

_____

_____

_____

Today's Prayer

Dear Lord,

I pray that You will give me the wisdom I need to know which gardens I am to be a part of. Help me to know if there are gardens that I need to leave, and if there are any, please give me strength and guidance on how to do it. If there are new gardens I'm about to enter and they are not aligned to Your will, please put a donkey in the road to stop me. I want to be where You want me to be.

In Jesus's name I pray, Amen.

Day 15

 ## Serving Everywhere, Every Day

Then these righteous ones will reply, "Lord, when did we ever see you hungry and feed you? Or thirsty and give you something to drink? Or a stranger and show you hospitality? Or naked and give you clothing? When did we ever see you sick or in prison and visit you?"
And the King will say, "I tell you the truth, when you did it to one of the least of these my brothers and sisters, you were doing it to me!"
Matthew 25:37–40

TODAY, YOU ARE who you are based on where and when you were born, the personality you were born with, the people and experiences who shaped your growth, and the collection of talents and gifts that God has given you. You are uniquely positioned in many gardens where God can use you to fulfill His plan.

Instead of thinking of how to serve God "somewhere

else," start by serving Him where you are. You do not have to create new ways to serve Him. Just look around and see all the mission fields He has already placed you in. Remember, if God had intended you to be a missionary in Africa, He would have shaped your birth, talents, desires, and circumstances in a way that aligned to that. Just because that is not your calling, doesn't mean you cannot serve Him in a significant way. He has made you and placed you exactly where He needs you to be in His magnificent plan. You simply need to bloom where you are planted.

Too often we think of "serving God" as big important things to be done. We view the sermon our pastor preaches, or the life of the missionaries we know, as really important acts of service, and they are. However, God has plans for all of us. In Ephesians 2:10, it says, "For we are God's masterpiece. He has created us anew in Christ Jesus, so we can do the good things he planned for us long ago." Good things come in many shapes and sizes. Some are small, but no less important. God prepared in advance the works for you and me, so don't belittle what you can offer as you bloom exactly as He has planned. There are so many ways to represent Jesus and serve Him every day. You can show His love and kindness in every encounter with every person.

One morning at work, I went down to get a cup of coffee. I was standing in line behind a woman I knew. I asked how she was doing, and she said, "It's been a rough month." She then shared that her dad had passed away unexpectedly. I had lost my mom about two years prior, and so I had this experience to draw on as I talked with her. It was not a long conversation, but I do believe that it was a divine appointment and an opportunity to show her Jesus's love and kindness.

Simply loving people as God intends us to is important. As it says in Matthew 25:37–40, God views us helping others the same as if we were actually helping Jesus. That's incredible! Anytime you take a minute to say a kind word to someone, it's as if Jesus were standing right there with them, receiving it as well. So cool!

It's also important to talk about Jesus with others. You can share what He's done in your life, how He's answered your prayers, and what He means to you. You can share the plan of salvation with those you love. There are so many ways to bloom, and in the coming days, we will explore ways you can do that in each garden you are placed in.

Reflection

1. Think back over the past few days. Describe a conversation or encounter you had where you had a chance to be kind and loving to someone.

_____

_____

_____

_____

_____

_____

2. Is there someone in your life right now who you know is in the midst of a difficult time? What can you do for them?

_____

_____

_____

_____

3. Think about a time when someone reached out in kindness to you. How did it make you feel?

_____

_____

_____

_____

4. Is there anything God is saying especially to you today as you read and think about this lesson?

_____

_____

_____

_____

Today's Prayer

Dear Father,

Thank You, Lord, for bringing so many people across my path to give me so many chances to show Your love and kindness to others. I pray that You will open my eyes and my heart to see each opportunity that You give me. It warms my heart to know that when I am kind to others, You are blessed as well.

In Jesus's name I pray, Amen.

Day 16

Actions Speak Louder than Words

By his divine power, God has given us everything we need for living a godly life. We have received all of this by coming to know him, the one who called us to himself by means of his marvelous glory and excellence.
2 Peter 1:3

IT'S ALWAYS EASIEST to care for the plants that are close to home—those in your house and those planted around your house. You don't have to go far to reach them. You have access to them every day. They depend on you to take care of them. Your family is like this too. You see them more than any other people—every day for most of us. They are close by and depend on you to care for them in many ways.

Jerusalem was the home of the disciples, and it was the first place where Jesus said to witness. Your family is your Jerusalem. If you are married, this may mean your spouse.

If you have a family, this will include your children. If you are single, it could mean your siblings and your parents.

Your family learns a lot by simply watching you. They see your beliefs and faith play out in your life each day. If you go to church every Sunday but are not living according to God's ways throughout the rest of the week, your family will be confused. They'll get a skewed understanding of what it means to be a Christian. Your strongest witness to your family is how you act in everyday circumstances. Do you give God credit for the good things that happen in your life? Do you respond to bad situations with a strong and faithful trust in God? Do you take the family's problems to God in prayer? Do you forgive them, just as God has forgiven you? Do you stick to what is right, even when it means you have to be hard on your kids? When you stand up for and behave according to your beliefs, and your life is consistent with your faith, it leaves a permanent impression on your family. They will notice, and they will remember it.

When my son was in college, he was making some poor choices. We could have brushed this off as "it's just a phase" and let it go. However, doing so would not have aligned with our beliefs. So, we had to make some hard decisions and allow him to bear the consequences of his actions. Throughout the ordeal, we constantly emphasized that we loved him, and while we had to take action, we did not want it to hurt our relationship. In the end, he paid the price for his decision, but he also saw an example of standing firm for your beliefs, and that's a lesson I see him apply in his life today.

At home, you are always on stage. When people know

you are a Christian, Jesus is on that stage with you. Who He is and how He is affecting your life is front and center for your family to see. Be sure they see the Jesus who saved you!

Reflection

1. Consider one of your latest encounters with someone in your family. Put Jesus in your place. Would He have said or done anything differently, or were you a good representative of Him?

_____

_____

_____

_____

2. Imagine that you are on trial for being a Christian. What evidence would your family see in your life that proves you are a Christian? What behaviors, habits, and actions would support this claim?

_____

_____

_____

_____

3. Who are the people in your family that see you all the time? How can you improve upon your daily living in

a way that strengthens their understanding of what it means to love and follow Jesus?

_____

_____

_____

_____

_____

4. Is there anything God is saying especially to you today as you read and think about this lesson?

_____

_____

_____

_____

_____

Today's Prayer

Dear Jesus,

Thank You for my salvation and for being with me always. I pray that Your love and light would shine through me and that others would be drawn to You as they see the amazing ways that You have changed me for the better. Lord, help my words and actions become beacons of hope that lead those around me to You.

In Your name I pray, Amen.

Day 17

~~~~ **Words Matter** ~~~~

---

*And you must love the Lord your God with
all your heart, all your soul, and with all your
strength. And you must commit yourselves whole-
heartedly to these commands that I am giving
you today. Repeat them again and again to your
children. Talk about them when you are at home
and when you are on the road, when you are
going to bed and when you are getting up.*
Deuteronomy 6:5–7

PEOPLE WHO LOVE gardening will often tell you that they believe talking to plants helps them grow. Some scientists
believe that talking to plants gives them more carbon dioxide, which they need to grow. The TV show *MythBusters*
did a study where they had separate greenhouses. In one
they played recordings of speech and music, and in the
other there was no sound. The silent greenhouse showed
the least amount of plant growth. Not conclusive, but it

does seem to support the claim that talking to plants does affect their growth.

While it's not 100 percent certain that talking to plants makes them grow faster, I can say with certainty that your family will have a much greater probability of coming to know Jesus if you talk to them about Him. Living out your faith is key and a strong witness to your family. It is also important that you *talk* to your family about God. You should not rely on someone else to tell your family about God and His amazing plan of salvation. Who are they going to trust more than you? Knowing and accepting Jesus is the most wonderful thing that has happened to you. It is the most important decision you will ever make and one that has put you on the path to eternal life. Sharing that with the family you love just makes sense.

My son, Brian, and his wife, Krista, have four young children, ages two to seven. Brian and Krista have spoken to their kids about Jesus since the beginning. They taught their children to pray at meals, and when Brian and Krista would pray "thank you for . . ." while the kids were learning to talk, the kids would yell out "Jesus!" They read stories from the Bible to them and say bedtime prayers. They listen to and sing worship songs with them in the car. They tell them how much God loves them, and I am sure that when the kids are old enough to understand, Brian and Krista will share the gospel with them.

My daughter, Jacquelyn, and her husband, Todd, have older children, ages ten to eighteen. They have accepted Jesus as their Lord and Savior, and their parents are now focused on teaching them to grow in their relationship with God. This includes praying together and doing devotionals with them to help them better understand how to live out their faith. One of their sons is a great swimmer, and he and Jacquelyn pray before each meet, and when he wins, he gives God the credit. They also have a tradition that when each child reaches a certain age, they will take them on a mission trip with the church. Todd and Jacquelyn are actively engaged with their children, helping them to strengthen their faith.

I am blessed to have two of our children following Christ and leading their families spiritually. However, I didn't always do this well with my own family, and maybe you didn't either. That's okay. God is still in control and may have been using others to reach your children. And, more importantly, it's not too late to begin! I wouldn't suggest you wake up tomorrow and start doing ten new spiritually focused things with your kids. However, I would suggest you pray about what those things could be and ask God to guide you to pick one to begin. You can make a huge difference in your children's lives, or if you don't have children, in the lives of the family members you interact with. Just like talking to a plant can help it grow, sharing the words of Jesus with the family around you can help them come to know Him and grow in their faith.

Reflection

1. Do you talk to your children or other family members about Jesus? If so, describe what you do and how it has impacted them. If you don't, reflect on why you don't—your fears, what gets in the way, and so forth.

_____

_____

_____

_____

_____

2. Name some ways you do or can bring Jesus to the fore-front of the relationship you have with your children, grandchildren, or other family members.

_____

_____

_____

_____

_____

3. What is something amazing God is doing in your life right now? Pick someone in your family to share that with.

_____

_____

_____

_____

_____

4. Is there anything God is saying especially to you today as you read and think about this lesson?

_____

_____

_____

_____

_____

_____

Today's Prayer

Dear Jesus,

Thank You for saving me! Thank You for sacrificing Your life so that I can have a relationship with God and have eternal life. I pray that You would help me to be better at talking about You with my children, grandchildren, and other family members. Use me to share the gospel to help them grow in their love for You and live out their faith in the world. Please give me practical ideas for how to do this.

In Your name I pray, Amen.

Day 18

The Most Important Thing to Talk About

For I am not ashamed of this Good News
about Christ.
It is the power of God at work, saving everyone
who believes—the Jew first and also the Gentile.
Romans 1:16

WE ARE CALLED to bear fruit for God. Ultimately, the goal is to bring others into a saving relationship with Jesus Christ. We may often contribute to the steps which lead a person to a fruitful life in Christ, and sometimes we are called to deliver the clear message of the gospel, helping them to cross that critical point in their lives. It's such a blessing when it happens, and yet for most of us, it's so hard to do.

Talking to your kids about Jesus when they are young is easy, as you are in control of their lives, and they generally believe anything you tell them (at least until about age five!). As your children get older, it becomes more challenging. The same is true of your extended family—your siblings, parents, nieces, nephews, and so on. Many Christians view witnessing to family members as a daunting and scary act. We are concerned about how they'll react, afraid that they'll make fun of us, or unsure that they will be open to it. I was definitely in that camp, and then God used a tough situation to teach me something about that.

My sister-in-law had cancer and was in hospice care. God put on my heart that I needed to go see her and talk to her about Him. I was so nervous about doing this. Even after I got to her house, I found myself procrastinating. I did finally do it, though. She told me that she believed in God and had accepted Jesus as her Savior. Praise the Lord! Later, at her funeral, her brother-in-law, who was a pastor, said that he had spoken to her as well (before I had arrived) and shared joyfully that she was saved. As I reflected on this, it appeared that my being there wasn't necessary for her to be saved. So, why did God send me?

I'm convinced it was for multiple reasons. First, it helped me grow. My fears of being laughed at or worse did not happen. No one made fun of me or asked me to not talk about Jesus. Secondly, I found it much easier to share after that. I told some of my other siblings the purpose of my visit and was able to naturally share my testimony with them. Turns out my family members were a lot more open to talking about God than I had thought. Third, I also shared what I was doing with my children and their spouses, asking them to pray for me and sharing with them what happened. Perhaps one day when faced with a similar situation, they'll remember my story and have the courage to do the same.

I don't know the full impact or reasons why God sent me to talk to my sister-in-law. God's plan is way too complex for any of us to understand. I do know that God wants as many to be saved as possible. He loves everyone and wants people to believe in His Son, accept Him as Lord of their lives, and spend eternity with Him. As you think about your family, you don't know how much time you have left with them. You may not have another year, month, week, or even a day. Don't wait. Tell your family about Jesus now. Share the greatest truth and the greatest gift with those you love the most.

The process is as simple as A-B-C. A = Accept that you are a sinner and have fallen short of God's glory. B = Believe that Jesus is God's Son, who died on a cross to take the punishment for your sins and then rose from the dead as our living Savior. C = Confess your sins, ask for God's forgiveness, and accept Jesus as your Savior and the Lord of your life. Praying these things to God is all it takes. Have you ever done this? If not, now could be the perfect time to do so! Don't wait any longer to experience the joy of knowing Jesus and having Him be the Lord of your life.

Reflection

1. List out a few people in your family who are not saved.

_____

_____

2. As you talk to people about Jesus, one of the most powerful ways to start is to simply share what He has done for you. How has having Jesus as your Savior changed you? How does He make a difference in your life? Jot down your personal story here.

_____

_____

_____

_____

_____

_____

3. Write your fears about sharing the gospel with anyone on your list. Then, turn them over to God and ask Him to help you overcome them. Pray for opportunities to share your story with those on your list above. Picture the joy you would feel in seeing them accept Jesus as their Savior.

_____

_____

_____

_____

_____

_____

4. Is there anything God is saying especially to you today as you read and think about this lesson?

_____

_____

_____

_____

_____

_____

Today's Prayer

Dear Jesus,

I am so grateful for the life I have in You. Jesus, having You as my Savior has not only given me the guarantee of eternal life but has given me an amazing life now. I experience Your love, grace, and peace in my life every day. You've blessed my life in many ways and have always been beside me during challenging times. I could not imagine living this life without You. Lord, this is such good news! Help me to be more willing to share it with members of my family. Please give me opportunities and the courage to open up about what You've done for me on the cross and the difference You have made in my life.

In Your precious name I pray, Amen.

Day 19

❧ Being a Christian 24/7 ❧

Instead, you must worship Christ as Lord
of your life. And if someone asks about your hope
as a believer, always be ready to explain it.
1 Peter 3:15

I LOVE A BOUQUET of roses, each looking much like the other. This reminds me of my circle of friends. After being a Christian for years, most of my friends are Christians also, and together we look like that bouquet of roses. We look and smell beautiful together, working in harmony with one another and helping each other grow in our faith.

I also love a bouquet of different kinds of flowers, and that makes me think of how we mix with a variety of people in our lives. Christian friends are important for fellowship and growth, but it's also important that we interact with others who are not saved so that we can influence their lives. Otherwise, it's like you staying in your backyard, enjoying and cultivating your own rose garden while ignoring the variety of blooms beyond your home that are in desperate need.

It is typically in the workplace that many of us interact with unsaved souls. Many people you work with do not go to church or have any Christian friends. It could be that you are the only Christian they will ever meet. If you don't work outside the home, your opportunity may lie at the gym you frequent or some other social circle you're in, like a mom's club or community group. At work or in these groups, you can show Jesus's love, shine for Him, and when opportunity knocks, become a part of His plan to save them.

I'd like to share a few stories from my work experiences. As you read the next few devotionals, if you don't work outside the home, think about how the lessons can be applied in other social circles you are a part of.

I work as a manager at a large company in Ohio. For a long time, I compartmentalized my life. I did not talk about or share my faith with those I worked with. Church on Sunday, work on Monday through Friday, and never the two shall meet! God, however, had other plans. It all started with a friend and colleague who worked in my department. My church was starting a new program that included a small group study. One day, shortly before we were to begin, I was having lunch with her. During our discussion, it became clear that she was struggling, and she said something to the effect of, "I don't know my purpose in life." Well, the Holy Spirit set alarm bells off in my head, and I quickly shared with her that our church was about to do a study on *The Purpose Driven Life* by Pastor Rick Warren.

Coincidence? I think not! A moment planned perfectly by God? Most definitely!

We agreed to do a study together alongside what I was doing at church. I thought this was kind of cool, as I'd never done anything faith-based at work up to this point. A small, personal study was a good place to start. Well . . . God had a little more in mind. Over the following few days, other people crossed my path who were in God's sights. Next thing I know, I'm leading a study with a group of five women. We met each week over lunch for the study, and it was amazing!

As I reflect on this story that happened over fifteen years ago, I am still amazed at what God does through us if only we are willing to step out for Him. I marvel at how God gave me the talents I needed to get the job that I had, and had my friend born at the time and place she was, and gave her the talents she had, to bring our lives to this inter-section in the workplace. Not to mention how the timing of that study at my church was also at just the right time, as was the timing of Rick Warren's birth and life path to write the study. God's plan is mind-boggling!

God has placed you in a garden somewhere—work and/or social circle—where He can and wants to use you. Remember, you are where you are because of so many fac-tors. It could be that right now as you are reading this, your garden is ripe for planting or watering. As Paul says in 1 Corinthians 3:6, "I planted the seed in your hearts, and Apollos watered it, but it was God who made it grow." Let God use you to share His wonderful love and grace with others, and then watch God at work!

Reflection

1. In what ways do you compartmentalize your life, keeping God out of your work or other activities?

_____

_____

_____

_____

2. Think about your workplace or groups you are a part of. How would you describe them through the spiritual eyes of God?

_____

_____

_____

_____

3. Create a list of names of people you interact with at work or other activities, who you know are unsaved. Begin praying for them and for an opportunity to be a part of God's plan to reach them.

_____

_____

_____

_____

4. Is there anything God is saying especially to you today as you read and think about this lesson?

_____

_____

_____

_____

_____

_____

Today's Prayer

Dear God,

I thank You for the people You have put in my path that don't know You. I pray that You will give me the courage and the opportunity to show them Your love. Help me to sow seeds of love, grace, and mercy. I specifically pray for (fill in the names of the people you wrote above). It would be a privilege to serve You in a small or big way to reach them.

In Jesus's name I pray, Amen.

Day 20

⪻⪻⪻ The Dandelion Effect ⪼⪼⪼

Now all glory to God, who is able, through his mighty power at work within us, to accomplish infinitely more than we might ask or think.

Ephesians 3:20

MANY SEE DANDELIONS as a pesky weed to remove. But have you ever seen an entire yard or field full of the yellow blooms or the white, puffy seed heads? They are beautiful! The one thing that we can agree on is that they spread easily. One dandelion flower can produce forty to one hundred or more seeds, and the blowing of the wind can spread them to sprout up in surrounding areas. They then create new flowers, which also turn to seed and blow even farther out. Thus, a field of dandelions is born. This is a great picture of how God can use one thing you do to seed another, and another, until an entire field of impact has been created by the one thing you did.

Like the dandelion, the *Purpose Driven Life* study I did with my friends at work produced more seeds and spread. One example was in the profound impact it had on that first co-worker I mentioned. She grew so much in her understanding of what God wanted of her, and shortly after this study, God led her to take a huge leap of faith. A few weeks after we finished the study, my friend learned that she was pregnant with her second child. She and her husband began to feel that God was asking her to stay home with her children. She was the primary breadwinner of the family, and this seemed completely illogical. However, God kept speaking to her, and after much prayer, she followed His will and quit her job to be with her children. At the same time, she and her husband joined a church, became involved in ministry, and began to impact other people's lives. I lost touch with my friend; however, I am confident that God used her and her husband to impact others for the kingdom. Just like the dandelion seeds, His plan spreads outward, each new seed growing new flowers of faith.

Other seeds were planted from my encounter with *The Purpose Driven Life*. I kept an extra copy on hand and gave it out on multiple occasions to those who God led me to, and I know it impacted their lives. After the initial study, I continued to have Bible studies with a few of the women. It also led me to a very special person who is now my best friend.

One day, I was walking past the desk of a coworker when I saw *The Purpose Driven Life* on her desk. I stopped in and invited her to attend our Bible study. She answered with an enthusiastic yes! This began her journey of building a real and authentic relationship with Jesus. It also led to an amazing friendship, and many, many years of Bible studies that have helped deepen her faith and mine. This is an incredible example of how being willing to be a part of God's plan touches not only the lives of many others but also blesses your own. It can start so small, like that tiny seed, and blossom into something amazing.

God may not call you to lead a Bible study; it could be something else entirely. He created you with different talents and gifts and has placed you in your own gardens. The key is to be open, have a desire to serve Him, and then wait for Him to provide the opportunity to plant that one small seed and watch it grow.

Reflection

1. Reflect on a time when you have seen the "dandelion effect" of God's work in people's lives.

---

2. What is a time when you served God in some way and it turned back into a blessing for your own life?

----

3. Knowing that God can turn small things into things with big impact, think and pray about whether there is something right now that you believe God would like you to do. Write down what it is and how you can take the first step.

----

4. Is there anything God is saying especially to you today as you read and think about this lesson?

_____

_____

_____

_____

_____

_____

_____

Today's Prayer

Dear Heavenly Father,

Your plans are so, so much more than we can comprehend. You can use the smallest of things to have such a big impact on the world. I pray that You will increase my sensitivity and openness to the little opportunities for me to sow or water a seed and watch You make it grow. I humbly submit to You and to the Holy Spirit to guide me and make me aware of them. Loving and serving You is my greatest desire.

In Jesus's name I pray, Amen.

Day 21

Be Like Jesus

Since God chose you to be the holy people he
loves, you must clothe yourselves with tender-
hearted mercy, kindness, humility, gentleness,
and patience. Remember, the Lord forgave you,
so you must forgive others.
Above all, clothe yourselves with love, which
binds us all together in perfect harmony.
Colossians 3:12–14

I HAVE LEARNED THERE are times when the thing God most needs me to do, is be like Jesus. What speaks to this is the fruits of the Spirit found in Galatians 5:22–23, which are love, joy, peace, patience, kindness, goodness, faithfulness, gentleness, and self-control. These are all things that God's Spirit can create in us, which help us to become more like Him. The world needs more people that emulate the characteristics found in those verses. We are all faced with choices every day in how we treat those around us. What we say and how we react to what others say and do is important. The more we rely on the Spirit to help us be like Jesus in those moments, the more beautifully we will bloom.

I've had situations that required me to take some difficult actions. Seeking God's direction and guidance in them has been crucial. Whenever I've had to deal with a difficult person, I rely on God to help me through it. I surrender to the Holy Spirit and let Him guide me to the right decisions and actions. I also always pray that the person will be able to weather the actions I've needed to take. I believe that God has placed me in specific roles at specific times to do what needed to be done when others would not do it.

I also saw this happen with my friend Linda. She was in a role at work for several years and became adamant against moving to anything new. She had a few opportunities she could have sought, but she didn't pursue them. Then, because of some changes being made at work, she was told she would be reassigned to another role. She felt this was unfair, and she was unhappy about it.

After being in the new role for a short while, she had a tragic situation in her team where one of her managers died unexpectedly. I believe that because of her relationship with God, she was in a much better position to help her team through this difficult time than her predecessor would have been. She prayed for them and was able to be the vessel for God to provide love and comfort to others. God needed her there. I believe we always need to be open to change, even when it's not what we want, because God may have an important task ahead that He needs you for.

In Ephesians 5:8–9 it says, "For once you were full of

darkness, but now you have light from the Lord. So live as people of light! For this light within you produces only what is good and right and true." God needs His people to be the light in a dark world. We need to be different than what the world expects. We need to be kind, loving, and patient with those who are not kind, loving, or patient with us. We need to have joy in our Savior in the midst of painful situations. We need to show others what Jesus is like by being like Him in how we think, talk, and behave in all situations in our lives. God needs us to stand out and stand up for His way of living. Let people see Jesus shining through you!

Reflection

1. What are some ways that you treat others like Jesus would?

_____

_____

_____

_____

2. How do you think being like Jesus affects those around you?

_____

_____

_____

_____

3. Jesus is our example to follow. Jot down some of His attributes that you aspire to emulate.

_____

_____

_____

_____

_____

4. Is there anything God is saying especially to you today as you read and think about this lesson?

_____

_____

_____

_____

_____

Today's Prayer

Dear Heavenly Father,

Thank You for coming to earth and showing us through Your Son's life how to live and treat others. I long to be more like Jesus. Please help me continue to grow more like Him, so that I may treat others as He would every day. I pray the Holy Spirit will continue to mold and shape me into His image.

In Jesus's name I pray, Amen.

Day 22

⤜⤜ Be the Light on the Hill ⤛⤛

You are the light of the world—like a city on a
hilltop that cannot be hidden.
No one lights a lamp and then puts it under a
basket. Instead, a lamp is placed on a stand,
where it gives light to everyone in the house.
In the same way, let your good deeds shine out for
all to see,
so that everyone will praise your heavenly Father.
Matthew 5:14–16

PICTURE AN INCREDIBLY beautiful garden. Flowers of all shapes, sizes, and colors bloom brightly—a true feast for your eyes. You are the owner of that garden, and you take loving care of it. And . . . you keep it a secret. You are the only one who sees it and knows about it. No one else is aware of this beautiful creation. What a terrible waste that would be! In some ways, that's what it's like when you know Jesus and are a beautiful daughter of the King, and no one knows. They don't get to see or understand who you really are.

Do people you interact with know you are a Christian? I hope there is plenty of evidence in your life that you are different, but do people think you are just a super nice person? Do they know where your love and kindness come from? Do they realize you are quick to forgive because you've been forgiven? Do they know it is from God that you draw your strength and joy? Is He given the credit for it all? For any of it?

It's important that people know that you are who you are because of Him. His love has taught you to love, and His sacrifice and forgiveness have made you a child of God. He is the source of your goodness. People need to know, and you need to tell them. Don't hide it or stay silent. Let them know that you are a Christian. Let your light shine.

Whenever I have someone new reporting into me at work, I take them through a series of get-to-know-you questions that we both answer. Some are work-centric, such as career desires, how they like to be coached, and so forth. Some are more personal. One question I ask is, "What do I want you to know about me?" I use this question to let them know that I'm a Christian. My hope is that when they see how I treat people, and it looks different than what they've seen in others, they will connect the two. This also lets them know they can come to me for prayer or personal help. I am motivated to live the way Jesus wants because I know that they know. I want them to have the right impression of what being a Christian looks like.

I once had an opportunity to go public in a big way. I was asked to speak at a women's leadership event with two hundred-plus people in attendance. They asked me to tell my life story in five minutes or less, mentioning the major events and influences. I simply couldn't do that without talking about my decision to follow Christ because it was the most important decision and the greatest influence of my life. So, I included it. Afterward, I had people who were Christians come up to me and tell me how impressed they were that I had the courage to share. My hope and prayer is that those who heard me would become more courageous about their own beliefs.

I used to think it was hard to serve God outside of church. It's really not. You just need to understand that it comes in many forms. It starts by letting Jesus's love and grace shine through you in how you treat people every day. Then, letting people know you are a Christian will help them understand why you are the way you are, and God will receive the glory He deserves.

Reflection

1. Do people at work or in your social circles know you are a Christian? If so, is that because you've told them or showed them, or both? If not, why is that?

_____

_____

_____

_____

_____

_____

2. What's an approach you could use to let people who don't know yet that you are a Christian?

_____

_____

_____

_____

3. How do you think people have changed (or will change) the way in which they interact with you once they know you are a Christian?

_____

_____

_____

_____

_____

4. Is there anything God is saying especially to you today as you read and think about this lesson?

_____

_____

_____

_____

_____

Today's Prayer

Dear God,

Thank You for giving Your only Son to die on the cross to take the punishment for my sins. Thank You for choosing me to believe and be adopted into Your family. I am not ashamed to be a Christian. My relationship with You is the most important thing in my entire life. Please help me to be courageous about letting others know.

In Jesus's name I pray, Amen.

Day 23

Serving in the Family of God

A spiritual gift is given to each of us so we can help each other.
To one person the Spirit gives the ability to give wise advice; to another the same Spirit gives a message of special knowledge. The same Spirit gives great faith to another, and to someone else the one Spirit gives the gift of healing.
1 Corinthians 12:7–9

EACH PART OF an apple tree plays an important role in the life of that tree. The roots gather water and nourishment from the soil. The trunk takes the water and feeds it into the rest of the tree. The leaves gather sunlight and convert it into energy through photosynthesis. The tree produces apples, which contain seeds that can be used to grow more trees. The church is like this. Each person plays a role in the health and growth of the church. Each person was designed by God to play a specific role. This results in a healthy and happy family of God, and one that multiplies into a larger family over time. The key to this is spiritual gifts.

Talents are natural abilities that God gives every person when they are born. Spiritual gifts are another type of talent that is given to those who have accepted Christ as their Savior. Once a person is saved, God gives them special gifts that are designed to help others in the family of God. First Corinthians 12:5–7 says, "There are different kinds of service, but we serve the same Lord. God works in different ways, but it is the same God who does the work in all of us. A spiritual gift is given to each of so that we can help each other."

As you read on in this passage, it shares what some of those spiritual gifts are and how they all fit together. They are also mentioned in Romans 12 and Ephesians 4. They include things such as teaching, serving, hospitality, scriptural discernment, and leadership. When everyone uses the gifts that God has given them, the result is a healthy congregation.

Just like talents, God selects and gives us our spiritual gifts. Your spiritual gifts are a special part of who you are. They are a critical part of God's plans to grow the church. As it says in 1 Corinthians 12:7, these gifts are given to us to *help each other.* Do you know what your gifts are? Maybe you are part of the root system, hidden underground, but vital to the nourishment of the church, perhaps through prayer. Maybe you have the gift of encouragement or discipleship, like the sun that is needed to help others grow in their walk with God.

If you don't know what your spiritual gifts are, there are several tests online that can help you discover what they are.

I encourage you to take one or talk to your pastor about it. Take the time to understand the gifts God has given you, and then, most importantly, apply them with your brothers and sisters in Christ.

If you don't know or aren't using your spiritual gifts, then your church family is missing out. If you are not serving, you are a missing piece of the puzzle that is needed to keep the church healthy and on mission. Applying the gifts God has given you will be rewarding and will help God's family—the church—to produce much fruit in furthering God's kingdom.

Reflection

1. What part do you currently play in the life of your church family? In what ways do you serve them?

_____

_____

_____

_____

2. Think about a typical Sunday morning at your church. How many different serving opportunities are there?

_____

_____

_____

_____

3. If you are not currently serving in the church in any way, what's stopping you from doing so, and how can you remove whatever obstacles are in your way to get started?

_____

_____

_____

_____

4. Is there anything God is saying especially to you today as you read and think about this lesson?

_____

_____

_____

_____

Today's Prayer

Dear Lord,

Thank You for Your holy church, and specifically, thank You for my church. Thank You for my pastor and how You have gifted him to lead our congregation. Thank You for all the others in the church who serve to make everything work smoothly, both out front and behind the scenes. I pray that You will guide me to understand my spiritual gifts and lead me to the work You have planned for me so that I can play my part.

In Jesus's name I pray, Amen.

Day 24

⤜⤜ Discover Your Spiritual Gifts ⤛⤛

But our bodies have many parts,
and God has put each part just where he
wants it.
1 Corinthians 12:18

EVERY SPIRITUAL GIFT and every activity done to serve the church is equally important. Going back to the apple tree analogy, all the parts are needed. No one can see the roots, but the tree will not grow without them. No one can see photosynthesis, but it's working, and the tree would die without it. As it says in 1 Corinthians 12:21, "The eye can never say to the hand, 'I don't need you!' The head can't say to the feet, 'I don't need you.'" An eye needs to be an eye, and a foot needs to be a foot; they cannot take each other's place, and they need each other for the body to function properly. Everyone is important, and everyone needs to play the role they were gifted to do. When it's all working as planned, apple trees blossom and bear much fruit, and so does the church.

God gave complementary spiritual gifts to my husband and I, which has made us an effective ministry team. One of my spiritual gifts is teaching. I love teaching children and taught Sunday school for many years. I can take Bible stories and truths and turn them into lessons and crafts that a six-year-old can understand. My husband doesn't have the gift of teaching. However, one of his spiritual gifts is discernment of the Scriptures. So as I prepared a lesson, I would often talk over the story with my husband, who could help me understand the meaning more deeply. This prepared my heart and thoughts to build the lesson. My husband also has the gift of serving, which has made him the perfect teacher's aide!

There are so many different gifts, each with a multitude of nuances. While I love teaching young children, I'm just not wired to teach teenagers. I've tried, and I was not good at it, nor did I enjoy it. I felt like a fish out of water. On the other hand, I've met some wonderful people who are amazing with teenagers, but they steer clear of the elementary kids! That's what is so great about God's plan—He gifts people precisely for specific roles or tasks, which when mixed all together, is exactly what is needed for the whole to be successful.

There is a statistic that says 20 percent of a congregation does all the work in the church. I hope that's not true in yours. If there are too few people serving, or people are not in the right roles, then the church and its effectiveness in reaching the lost will be negatively impacted. If all God's people exercise the spiritual gifts He has given them, then the church would be a thriving garden where the saved are encouraged, growing, and joyful, and the unsaved are welcomed, loved, and coming to know Jesus.

If you are already serving, love what you are doing, and are good at it, then you are likely using one of your spiritual gifts. If you are serving in church in ways that are not aligned with your spiritual gifts, two things happen. First, you are likely unfulfilled because you are trying to do something you weren't built for. Secondly, you are taking someone else's ministry. There is someone in your church who has the right spiritual gift to do what you are struggling to do, and you could be in the way. Take time to discover your spiritual gifts and then work with your ministry leaders to get plugged into the right place. You will find joy in it, your church family will benefit, and your church will be one step closer to working the way God intended.

Reflection

1. Why is understanding and exercising your spiritual gifts in the church so important?

_____

_____

_____

_____

_____

_____

2. Who in your church excels at how they serve, and what spiritual gifts are they using?

_____

_____

_____

_____

3. What are your spiritual gifts? Find out if you don't know! How are you applying them? Or, if you aren't yet, what are some ways you could get started?

_____

_____

_____

_____

4. Is there anything God is saying especially to you today as you read and think about this lesson?

_____

_____

_____

_____

_____

Today's Prayer

Dear God,

Thank You for Your amazing plan for the church. Thank You for the spiritual gifts that You give to Your children. I pray that we will all discover them and use them to make our congregation stronger so that our church will be a place where people are encouraged and Your kingdom thrives.

In Jesus's name I pray, Amen.

Day 25

⇜⇜ Don't Be Too Firmly Planted ⇝⇝

"My thoughts are nothing like your thoughts,"
says the LORD. "And my ways are far beyond
anything you could imagine."
Isaiah 55:8

AT ONE TIME, we had many hosta plants around our home. As they matured and grew, they became dense. So, we needed to transplant some of them. Transplanting is good for the plants you leave behind and allows you to grow new ones somewhere else in your yard. God wants you to bloom in the church in which He has planted you. He wants you to use your talents and spiritual gifts to serve. There may, however, come a time when He needs to transplant you to a different garden. He may have another church that needs you even more.

I grew up believing that we were to stay loyal to our local church. My parents went to the same church for over sixty years. They never entertained leaving. There is nothing wrong with that if that's what God wants you to do. My husband and I joined a church in Macedonia, Ohio, which became our church home for several years. We know that God planted us there to be fertilized with His truths and to grow spiritually. It was there that we both became true followers of Christ, deepened our faith and understanding of the Bible, and built great friendships with a group of believers, who became true family to us. We became aware of our spiritual gifts and talents and put them to work. We were tightly integrated and serving in many ways. I felt that I could never move away from Macedonia, as I could never leave my church family.

Then, a strange thing happened. Through my work, an opportunity came up that would require us to move across the country. It was a great opportunity, and one I was seriously considering. This, of course, brought up the issue of leaving our church. While there was a time that this would have been a deal-breaker, by the time we discussed the idea, God had prepared us to be okay with it, in His perfect timing and in His perfect ways. More than anything, we wanted to live according to *His* will. Once we accepted the idea that we would and could leave our church if it was God's will, the work opportunity dissipated, but it became clear to us that He did want us to leave our church.

So, we left and went on a journey with God that eventually led us to a neighboring community. And amazing things happened there. My husband quickly moved into a high-level position in the church (something he had never done before) and had many opportunities to influence the church leaders. He also had the opportunity to help a fellow brother in Christ. He played a key role in bringing resolution to a difficult situation in this person's family. God gave my husband great wisdom in how to resolve the problem. I believe God placed and used my husband to help this man and his family. And if we had stayed too deeply rooted in our previous church, he wouldn't have even been there to be used by God.

God is looking for people who want to follow His will, no matter what. When you submit to His will and sacrifice your own desires, you give God permission to use you in His plans. If you do this, be ready for some tough choices, a few surprises, and a very fulfilling journey.

Reflection

1. Surrendering to God's will in everything is difficult, but so rewarding. Describe a time when God used you in a surprising way as a result of surrendering to His will.

_____

_____

_____

_____

2. Describe a time when your surrender to God's will required you to sacrifice your own desires.

_____

_____

_____

_____

3. Is there anything in your life that you are holding on to tightly (i.e., "I could not imagine ever changing this")? How might that be hindering God's work in your life?

_____

_____

_____

_____

4. Is there anything God is saying especially to you today as you read and think about this lesson?

_____

_____

_____

_____

Today's Prayer

Dear God,

Following Your will is the deepest desire of my heart. I know there are areas of my life that I don't even realize I have not submitted to Your will. Right now, I surrender every aspect of my life to You—my family, my job, my church, everything—and ask that Your will be done in every nook and cranny of my life. I love You, Lord, and look forward to being on the path that You have planned for me and being a part of Your plan.

In Jesus's name I pray, Amen.

Day 26

⟫⟫ God Works in Miraculous Ways ⟪⟪

*It was by faith that Abraham obeyed when God
called him to leave home and go to another land
that God would give him as his inheritance.
He went without knowing where he was going.*
Hebrews 11:8

ALL LIFE ON earth is connected. The ecosystem of our planet
is truly amazing. Think about a single forest. Trees grow
and provide oxygen, shelter, and food for the animals
within it. Animals provide carbon dioxide that the trees
need to live. Insects help to propagate more plants through
pollination. Animals die, and as their bodies decompose,
they enrich the soil so that it can produce more vegetation.
It's all interconnected.

Just like an ecosystem, all Christian churches in the
world are connected through Jesus. We all share the same
Savior, the same heavenly Father, and have the Holy Spirit
within us. We all share in our belief that Jesus is the Son of
God, and that he came to earth, took the punishment for

our sins by dying on the cross, and then came back to life three days later. We are one magnificent, interconnected church body. God has taught my husband and me a lot about this over the years. We have had a chance to attend many different churches as God continued to move us. He took my husband and me on another interesting mission to a different church, and like the first one, how He used us was incredible and unexpected. Because my husband had a key role in the church we were attending, we assumed God was going to have us there for some time. We were wrong. Again, we felt God calling us to leave. Moving from church to church was hard, and at times I had my doubts. God led me to the story of Abram. God asked him to go without giving him a lot of clarity as to why, and he lived as a nomad for several years. I felt a bit like that. God was asking us to once again pick up our tent and go, without giving us a clear understanding of why. However, after seeing how He used us the first time, I knew I could trust that He had a plan.

This time, God led us to a new church plant that was meeting in a high school, and we immediately believed that we were meant to be there. We enjoyed the preaching, joined a small group, my husband became a trustee, and I began teaching. We were settling in. However, we felt that God had us there for a specific reason that was not yet revealed to us. Then, unbeknownst to us, a piece of the puzzle fell into place when we were asked to go on a Mexican vacation with two dear friends of ours. At some point during the vacation, our friend mentioned that their church, which was also newer, was struggling, as they had lost their pastor. They were meeting at the local YMCA. My husband suggested that we ought to merge, as they had a location without a pastor and we had a pastor without a permanent location. It was a passing comment, nothing serious.

About two months later, my husband and I were talking about the fact that it was still not clear to us why God had us at this church, and then the phone rang. It was our friend letting us know that they had decided to close their church. He wanted to let us know before they informed the YMCA to see if our pastor would be interested in moving in. We hung up and immediately praised God, as we could see this specific thing that God had used us for. Long story short, our church did move to the YMCA, a badly needed permanent place that enabled them to grow and reach more people for God.

Your church is a vital part of your Christian life, and serving God and your church family is important. God's church is not just one place or one building; it's the family of all Christians everywhere. I don't believe He will call many people to leave one church to go to another, but we mustn't hold too tightly to anything, even our church. In the end, following God's will is the most important thing, no matter where it takes you.

Reflection

1. Describe a time when you've seen God use you or others through a series of incidents that seemed insignificant at the time but when strung together led to something amazing.

_____

_____

_____

_____

_____

2. Consider that the church is all God's children—His entire family. How does belonging to that church make you feel?

_____

_____

_____

_____

_____

3. What if God led you to leave your church? How easy or hard would that be?

_____

_____

_____

_____

4. Is there anything God is saying especially to you today as you read and think about this lesson?

_____

_____

_____

_____

_____

_____

Today's Prayer

Dear God,

Thank You for the many Christians in my life and for Christians all over the world who make up Your church. I pray today for those churches that are persecuted, those that are struggling, and those that are flourishing. May they all keep You at the center of everything they do. I pray that Your will be done in my life, in every aspect of my life, including serving in the church You've chosen me to be a part of.

In Jesus's name I pray, Amen.

Day 27

ᨳᨮᨮ Watering God's Gardens ᨮᨮᨮ

They are being tested by many troubles, and they are very poor. But they are also filled with abundant joy, which has overflowed in rich generosity. For I can testify that they gave not only what they could afford, but far more. And they did it of their own free will. They begged us again and again for the privilege of sharing in the gift for the believers in Jerusalem.
2 Corinthians 8:2–4

EVERYONE KNOWS THAT if you don't water a plant, it dies. Some plants, like trees and forests, require a lot of water. A newly planted tree needs twenty gallons of water weekly to grow. Rainforests by the equator receive more than eighty inches of rain annually. For God's Word to grow across the world, it needs a lot of watering—a lot more than one person can handle. We all need to do our part.

The Great Commission (Matt. 28:19) is to "go and make disciples of all the nations." In Acts 1:8, it says, "And you will be my witnesses, telling people about me everywhere—in Jerusalem, throughout Judea, in Samaria, and to the ends of the earth." I used to interpret this as meaning that *I* needed to go—I needed to be a missionary and take the Word to other countries. I have a different perspective on that now because I realized that we can't all go. However, we all need to play a part in reaching the entire world for Christ. There are many ways to do that, with three key ones being to pray, give, and encourage those who do go.

God has not wired me to be an overseas missionary. God designs each of us to bloom in our own ways. He's shaped me in a way that enables me to further His kingdom through my giving. When and where I was born, and the talents and experiences He has given me, has led me to become a successful businesswoman making a good income. I've come to understand that using some of my money to support overseas ministries is how God fits me into His plans to reach the world.

God has gifted many people to go and share the gospel, and He's gifted many of us to do other things that help to provide the funds for others to go. Financial support is key for organizations to reach the unsaved around the world. Giving to support them is one way we can fulfill our commission to take the gospel "to the ends of the earth."

Understanding the importance of financial support for spreading the gospel has taught me to think about my job and my work as an important part of God's plan to provide "water" for growing His kingdom. It's important to put our jobs in the right perspective. For example, if someone were to ask me when I plan to retire, I would tell them when God tells me to. It's not my choice. Who am I to say when I should stop working, which in turn would mean fewer funds to support the church and other Christian ministries? I'd hate to think that quitting when I wanted to would result in less being done in the ministries I support, and in turn, fewer people coming to know Jesus as their Savior. So, I will wait until God calls me to retire, as I will be confident that when He does, He is ready for me to move into a different part of His plan.

As a member of God's family, you have a part to play in fulfilling the Great Commission. Perhaps giving to a ministry is a way to fulfill your part. There are so many different ones out there, and I encourage you to pray and seek one that speaks to your heart. Even just a little giving can help. It takes twenty gallons a week to keep that tree alive. There are sixteen cups in a gallon, so if 320 people each pour one cup, that tree will stay alive for one more week. If hundreds of people give a little, it will add up, and God will use it to bear fruit around the world. You can be one of those people.

Reflection

1. Every penny given to God's work can be used. How does thinking about your family's income as an important part of God's plan change the way you think about your job or your spouse's?

_____

_____

_____

_____

2. Don't let the government or your own desires decide when you and/or your spouse should stop working. Let God guide you to the right time. How does this make you feel?

_____

_____

_____

_____

3. How do you feel about where you give? Is there a current need that God is pressing on your heart? If so, what's stopping you?

_____

_____

_____

_____

4. Is there anything God is saying especially to you today as you read and think about this lesson?

_____

_____

_____

_____

Today's Prayer

Dear God,

I am grateful that You have a place for me in Your plans to reach the "ends of the earth." You've provided finances that enable me to help support those who go and share the gospel to other nations. Help me to remember that even a small amount helps as it is added up with others who do the same. Please give me your wisdom and guidance on which ministry to give to.

In Jesus's name I pray, Amen.

Day 28

Prayer Changes Everything

---

*Confess your sins to each other and pray for each
other so that you may be healed. The earnest
prayer of a righteous person has great power and
produces wonderful results.*
James 5:16

MATTHEW 13:24-29 TELLS the parable of the "wheat and
weeds," where a farmer planted good seeds in his field
but at night his enemy came and planted weeds amongst
the wheat. As people around the world seek to sow God's
love and share the gospel, the enemy, Satan, is sowing
weeds to choke it out. Thankfully, God has given us the
weed killer needed to remove Satan's evil work: prayer!

Prayer is a powerful weapon against the evil forces that
are desperately trying to stop the gospel from spreading.
Remember, it is a spiritual battle that is being fought, a war
raging for the soul of each person. Prayer is a crucial part
of God's plan. Ephesians 6:12 says, "For we are not fight-
ing against flesh-and-blood enemies, but against evil rulers

and authorities of the unseen world, against mighty powers in this dark world, and against evil spirits in the heavenly places."

It then goes on to describe the armor of God we should be wearing each day. Once we have the full armor on, verse 18 tells us what to do: "Pray in the Spirit at all times and on every occasion. Stay alert and be persistent in your prayers for all believers everywhere." To win the spiritual battle all around us, we need to be praying for God's people around the world. The phrase "stay alert" also emphasizes the urgency in doing so.

The verse says to pray "on every occasion." There are so many ways to pray for those carrying the gospel to the world. You can pray for their spiritual needs—closeness with God and a boldness to share His love and message. You can pray for their physical and practical needs—safety, finances, materials, people, and other resources. You can pray for their emotional needs—encouragement, joy, perseverance, and companionship.

We are all in this spiritual battle. But are you actually "in it," or are you watching from the sidelines? Jesus asks you to be in it! Start praying for your brothers and sisters in Christ in their fight to bring the gospel to others. This includes those you know, such as your pastor, teachers within your church, Christian friends, and your church missionaries or supported ministries. You can also pray for those you don't know around the world who are trying to further God's kingdom. I would suggest you start by first asking Him to reveal a location in the world He'd like you to pray for. Then begin praying for the Christians in that country regularly. Do some research on what is happening with the spreading of the gospel in that country to identify specific things you can pray for. Then, watch God at work as He wins souls in the country you are praying for.

Reflection

1. In what ways do you already pray for those who share the gospel with others?

_____

_____

_____

_____

_____

2. Do you feel like you are helping in the spiritual battle, or are you more on the sidelines?

_____

_____

_____

_____

_____

3. Pray to God and ask Him to place a country on your heart to pray for. Write it down, along with one or two things you'll do to get started in praying for them.

_____

_____

_____

_____

4. Is there anything God is saying especially to you today as you read and think about this lesson?

_____

_____

_____

_____

Today's Prayer

Dear Mighty God,

I want to be an effective soldier for You in the spiritual battle raging around me. Help me to ensure that I'm wearing Your armor every day—truth, righteousness, readiness to share the gospel, faith, salvation, and Your Word. I pray for those around the world who risk their lives to share their faith with others. Protect them and give them the opportunities they so desire to win others to Your side. Help me also to have more boldness in my life to share Your love and the gospel with others.

In Jesus's name I pray, Amen.

Day 29

In the Desert

Pharaoh's chief cup-bearer, however,
forgot all about Joseph,
never giving him another thought.
Genesis 40:23

THERE HAVE BEEN times when God's work in my life and how He used me to contribute to His plan was crystal clear, and it was awesome! Something that used to bother me was when I would go for long periods where I felt God wasn't using me to do anything remarkable. I would beat myself up trying to understand why. Was there something wrong with my relationship with Him that was causing Him not to use me? Was I too caught up in my own desires that I was not following His will? Was I simply not listening or seeing the opportunities He put in front of me? Then, one day, I realized I was in good company.

In the story of Joseph, there were stretches of time between the amazing things he did. For example, in Genesis 41:1, it says, "two full years later." This was the time from when the cupbearer and baker were released from prison after Joseph interpreted their dreams to when Pharaoh had his dreams and the cupbearer remembered what Joseph had done for him. There is no mention of anything significant that happened during those two years. Joseph had asked the cupbearer to "please remember me and do me a favor when things go well for you. Mention me to Pharaoh, so he might let me out of this place." But the cupbearer forgot him. It's possible that some great things happened in those two years. It's also possible that Joseph just lived out his life each day doing ordinary things.

I realize now that it's kind of ridiculous to think that God should be using me (or any of us) in big, visible ways all the time. That's simply pride and arrogance speaking. Here's what I do know, though. While Joseph was in prison for two years, did he still love the Lord? Yes! Did he still treat people with kindness? Yes! Was he available to be used by God? Yes! Was he used by God in many ways he was unaware of? Absolutely! No matter what is going on, even when we are not seeing God use us, we can continue to grow in our relationship with and our love for God.

The point here is that there will be times in our lives when we become aware of an amazing way in which God has used us to fulfill a part of His plan. Rejoice in those. Write them down so you don't forget them. Then, there will be in-between times when you are still being used by God, but it may not be as apparent to you. That does not mean He is not at work. And the small stuff matters just as much for two reasons. First, if a small thing you do results in just one person being moved closer toward a relationship with Jesus, it's a *big* thing! Secondly, remember the dandelion effect? Think about the people in Billy Graham's life who influenced his salvation or started him on the road to his ministry. What they may have done could have been very small, but in the end, it resulted in God using a person to save thousands of people. So, just keep living according to God's will for your life—love God, love others, and continue to bloom where He has planted you.

Reflection

1. Think about Joseph in prison for two years waiting to be remembered. In what ways do you think he continued to show his love for God and others while there?

_____

_____

_____

_____

2. In what ways have you shown God's love and kindness to others this week? Know that this, too, is an important part of God's plan for your life and for those around you.

_____

_____

_____

_____

3. Whenever you experience a stretch of time when you don't *feel* you are doing anything for God, what can you do to remember He's still at work in you and that you are still part of His plan?

_____

_____

_____

_____

4. Is there anything God is saying especially to you today as you read and think about this lesson?

_____

_____

_____

_____

Today's Prayer

Dear Heavenly Father,

I know that I am a part of Your plan. You use me when I'm open and willing, and You even use me when I'm not aware. I've seen You do amazing things through me and others. There are times when I feel like I'm not being used, but I am sure that is not the case. Thank You for all the ways You've allowed me to be part of Your glorious plan!

In Jesus's name I pray, Amen.

Day 30

～ Let's Bloom! ～

For we are God's masterpiece.
He has created us anew in Christ Jesus,
so we can do the good things he planned for us
long ago.
Ephesians 2:10

WE'VE COVERED A lot of territory in the past twenty-nine days. We explored how God has created and shaped us into the people we are today. We spent a little time talking about how important it is to know His will for our lives and how to discern it. We also explored the many gardens in our lives that represent the mission fields God has planted us in to bloom for Him and His kingdom.

The general message of this devotional is twofold. First, each of us needs to accept who we are—God's masterpiece. God has orchestrated our birth and our life perfectly to grow us into the people we are today, beautiful flowers in His marvelously planned garden. Secondly, He has a plan for us "to do the good things He planned for us long ago." There are opportunities to demonstrate and share our love and faith in Jesus in all areas of our lives. He placed us in many different gardens—different areas of our lives where we can serve Him every day. Our gardens—home, work, social circles, church, and the world—are all ripe for planting and watering seeds of kindness, love, and faith.

Some flowers bloom quickly in the spring and fade fast. Others take longer to bloom and last all summer long. If you were to try to apply everything covered in this devotional, chances are you'd be like that fast-blooming, fast-fading flower, as you may become overwhelmed. So take it slowly. My hope and prayer is that some aspect of the last twenty-nine days resonated with you. Whichever day spoke to you the most is a good place to start.

A verse that nicely sums up what we've been talking about is John 15:16, and I'll end with this. Jesus says, "You didn't choose me. I chose you. I appointed you to go and produce lasting fruit, so that the Father will give you whatever you ask for, using my name."

God chose you! He has selected *you* to be part of His eternal kingdom and to participate in His plan on earth to bring others into the kingdom. He has appointed you to specific gardens to bear eternal fruit—helping others to seek and find Him so that they can have eternal life. And, lastly, you can ask for God's help directly as you look to bloom more fully in any of your gardens. It is a prayer He will definitely answer.

As we end our time together, I hope this devotional has shown you that you are an amazing, beautiful flower, and I pray that you will begin to bloom more fully in all of the gardens of your life. God bless you!

Reflection

1. As you think back over the past thirty days, what has resonated with you?

_____

_____

_____

_____

2. What garden or gardens in your life do you feel called to bloom more fully in? What is one thing you can do to get started?

_____

_____

_____

_____

3. If there is just one thing you want to remember from what God has taught you in the past thirty days, what is it? Write this down somewhere and put it in a place where you can be reminded of it regularly.

_____

_____

_____

_____

4. Is there anything God is saying especially to you today as you read and think about this lesson?

_____

_____

_____

_____

_____

_____

Today's Prayer

Dear God,

Thank You for the lessons You've taught me in the past thirty days. I know that I am Your masterpiece. You created me and love me. You've placed me in the paths of many people. I want to touch others in my gardens with Your love and grace. Thank You for choosing me and for making me part of Your amazing plan.

In Jesus's name I pray, Amen.

Order Information

To order additional copies of this book, please visit
www.redemption-press.com.
Also available on Amazon.com and BarnesandNoble.com
or by calling toll-free 1-844-2REDEEM.